Asking Questions

Asking Questions

A Challenge to Fundamentalism

by

Bahíyyih Na<u>kh</u>javání

GEORGE RONALD
OXFORD

GEORGE RONALD, Publisher
46 High Street, Kidlington, Oxford, OX5 2DN

British Library Cataloguing in Publication Data

Nakhjavani, Bahiyyih
   Asking questions: a challenge to fundamentalism
   1. Bahai doctrine
   I. Title
   297.93.

ISBN 0–85398–314–3

Contents

To
Peter Khan and Mona Greiser
because they were the first ones to ask the questions

Introduction

This book came about as a result of wondering about the danger of fundamentalist thinking and its relationship to the act of writing. Ironically enough, in spite of all one's poetic inclinations to the contrary, the act of writing, with its necessary reductionism and the concomitant implication that there should be a reader, suggests a tendency towards the fundamentalist pose which originally struck me as so dangerous and which has its roots in the oldest traditions of scholarship and priestcraft. So despite all appearances, this book is not only a sanctimonious exploration of these themes, but simultaneously a self-questioning of literary forms. It would not only be ironic, therefore, but in very poor taste if any of the ideas expressed in the following pages should mistakenly convey to the reader a fixed or final point of view. They were written as essays rather than as chapters, and if their being read sequentially conveys any 'thesis' it should be that the attempt to polish an idea is not the same as the desire to finish it.

I offer this book, therefore, to any readers who, like me, are disturbed by fundamentalist attitudes and seek creative solutions rather than dogmatic assertions about their cause. In particular, I offer it to Bahá'ís who because of the basic precepts of their Faith one might expect to be among the first to look for such creative solutions.

From the earliest days of its inception and during the most recent decade of its history the Bahá'í community in Iran has been at the mercy of one of the most virulent forms of religious fundamentalism. But certainly this community has not been the only victim. The century and a half which has elapsed since the founding of the Bahá'í Faith has spawned fundamentalism in political as well as religious forms all over the so-called civilized world. Totalitarianism, fascism, terrorism are only a few of the frightening 'isms' that have swept through our century. The industrialized nations have been just as vulnerable as those of the Third World to the lure of absolutist theories of both revolution and solution for the moral, economic and political degeneration of society. We seem to have spent the twentieth century throwing out all the absolutes – about God, about government, about family, about education – and replacing these with as many disturbing substitutes. Nietzsche claimed that God was dead just over one hundred years ago but if there is one lesson we might have learnt at the end of the twentieth century it is that Nietzsche's God might have had an afterlife for He seems to be taking a terrible revenge.

Fundamentalism, for my purposes in these essays, consists of that dogmatic attitude on the part of the adherent of any ideology, whether religious or political, that makes for a rigidity of attitude, a narrowness of vision and an unrelieved intolerance towards differing points of view. As a writer, it seems to me that drama has the greatest potential for undermining that fundamentalist position simply because polemic does not constitute great art, and I have therefore consistently searched for episodes in Bahá'í history that have the potential of being highly dramatic. As a Bahá'í, I am particularly interested in looking at the religious habits which have given rise to fundamentalist thinking because these habits, interestingly enough, also constitute richly dramatic material. The essays, therefore, reflect such themes as the traditional and confining attitude towards intellectual investigation, towards women and towards religious law. They are concerned with the divorce of ordinary people from the creative Word, which casts a patriarchal mystique around learning or scholarship, and they explore our tendency to look for interpreters and lean towards 'priestcraft'. Finally, they question our habits of blind instinct towards rebellion and subversion to which all these other tendencies have given rise.

For a Bahá'í, the essential truth at the heart of all religions is one. This is a point of unity to be stressed, to be invoked, to be continually rediscovered. What may be less easy to identify is whether or not our religious habits of mind, which arise in part from the social as well as spiritual teachings of the prophets, are the same as these essential truths. It is easy to mistake a religious habit for a spiritual attitude. It may be one of the unique contributions of the Bahá'í Cause to the religious history of mankind that we are called upon to recognize this difference and learn from it.

What is there in the teachings and history of the Bahá'í Faith to assuage the particular ills of fundamentalism in our age? How can we Bahá'ís guard against blind and 'idle imitations' in our own spiritual attitudes? How did the history of the Bahá'í Faith dramatize this struggle? How do the philosophical principles reflected in the dynamism of the Covenant of Bahá'u'lláh provide an armour for the human heart and mind to guard it from these habits of narrowness, rigidity and intolerance?

The following essays are constructed upon a few such questions. They are a personal exploration of Bahá'í history, through a personal interest in the genre of dramatic literature, in order to ponder over what has been different or is the same in our response to this latest religion from God. They are reflections on whether religious habits are immutable or might be changed. They are a meditation on what might be intrinsic to this Faith that both teaches us about the dangers and guards us against the tendencies of fundamentalist habits of mind. They tell stories in the attempt to write down thoughts.

1

Asking Questions

Do we have an innate desire to ask questions or is interrogation something we need to learn, to have stimulated? If questions are the means by which one stirs the passive mind and awakens the soul, how can they be asked so as to alert us to passionate inquiry rather than providing us with false choices? Why do we sometimes fear questions? Or is it the answers that we fear? And how can we guard against questions that coerce, that manipulate? Can questions freely asked tap the vast resources of spiritual, intellectual and emotional power in spite of being subject to contingency, as answers surely are?

The definition of a Bahá'í is, in a sense, one who believes in the power of questions. How else can one approach anything so dazzling as a Revelation and avoid blindness? Since it is in the nature of light to cast shadow, we can learn of it only by shielding our eyes. And since it is in the nature of darkness to cast nothing at all, we should distinguish from the outset the difference between the darkness which denies and the shadow that depends. Any study of the Bahá'í teachings requires that we recognize shadows to be our means of inquiry, shadows to be the language we construct, the images we comprehend. The areas of shadow are where the questions arise, where we see sharp contrasts and grapple with contradictions. That is where we can begin to define the shape of principles that would otherwise blind us.

'I love to lose my selfe in a mystery', wrote Sir Thomas Browne over three centuries ago, 'to pursue my reason to an *o altitudo* . . .' The mystery of God for this scholar was, as he puts it, 'wonderful in what we perceive but far more in what we comprehend not, for we behold him but asquint upon reflex or shadow.'[1]

In this century, when we have been called the 'generation of the half-light',[2] Sir Thomas Browne's definition of how we perceive the great mysteries of life 'asquint upon reflex or shadow' seems even more pertinent. Where there is a particularly bright source of light the shadows often seem to multiply and grow more dense. It takes great courage to recognize what is meant by the 'half-light', to live with its ambiguities and question them. It is therefore fitting that we begin to probe those areas where light and darkness overlap. To be a student of the Bahá'í Faith is to be one who has the courage to question the 'half-light' in which one dwells.

Perhaps we should first look squarely at the confusion that arises over the relative values we place on questions and answers. Chekhov wrote to his publisher on this point, warning against confusion between the solution of a problem and the correct posing of a question. He suggested that only the second is obligatory for the artist. For example, no problems are solved in *Anna Karenina* or in *Eugin Onegin* but the works are satisfactory because the questions in them are correctly posed. The same distinction applies to Bahá'í teachings as to great art. It is tempting to assume that the Faith is offering us answers when in fact what it is doing is helping us to pose the correct questions. We naively perceive questions as 'doubt' and answers as 'certitude' and assume, rather glibly, that just by being Bahá'ís we have all the longed-for answers to the imponderable questions of our age. We forget that it is the Revelation of Bahá'u'lláh that has unleashed these questions upon us over the last century and a half. It is actually His principles – of the relativity of truth and the progressive nature of spiritual evolution – that have caused such revolutions in men's thinking and set into motion such questions in the minds of scientists and housewives alike. This Cause has questioned the very basis of our rooted assumptions and requires of us the courage, even the heroism, to question, through each of its principles, our most secret and instinctive selves.

There are nineteen months in the Bahá'í calendar and one of them is actually called Questions, but there is no month of Answers. Clearly, we need to redefine what we mean by questions, then, for they do not necessarily lead to any conclusive answers. Rather they lead to an openness of mind, a humility of response and readiness of apprehension that finds resolution rather than solutions and which can rest as easily with paradoxes as with peace.

It should not be a surprise to us, therefore, to discover among the exalted names of God ones that leave many questions unanswered: the Unseen, the Inaccessible, the Unknowable, the Cleaver, the Withholder, the Concealer, the Impenetrable Mystery. Nor should we wonder when we read in *The Hidden Words* that 'souls shall be perturbed as they make mention of Me. For minds cannot grasp Me nor hearts contain Me.'[3] There are in the mystical writings of Bahá'u'lláh trees beyond which there is no passing, seas which are unfathomably shoreless, and once in a mysterious while a voice that can be heard 'from the inmost shrine: "Thus far and no farther" '.[4] It depends on which questions we ask, therefore, whether we might apprehend the city of certitude by means of subtle fragrances from the distance of a thousand leagues.

It could be said of course that the history of the human race, from one point of view, is the history of the wrong questions being asked. Whether transubstantiation is a matter worth burning for, whether you love the lady or go to war with the lord, whether invisible spirits rush about in your veins or the blood of menstruating women will defile you – all are quite pointless questions however entertaining. Literature is choked with them. 'To be or not to be' is a question that was guaranteed to lead Hamlet nowhere at all for the duration of five fascinating acts. Whether we have freewill or suffer from predestination keeps whole companies of fallen angels trapped in Milton's hell in Book II of *Paradise Lost*. And of course the good old 'Art v. Nature' questions have kept writers fiddling for centuries since Rome burned. In our own century we have asked questions so ludicrous as to drive millions of people into wholesale slaughter in concentration camps; and in the present day, in our courts of law, in our statutes of governance, we protect the rights of women as mothers on the basis of a definition of equality that implies the possibility of pregnant men.

Frivolity aside, however, the most important question facing us at this uncertain juncture in the history of human civilization is whether or not we can begin to ask the correct questions soon enough to halt the deadly consequences of asking the wrong ones for so long. Or perhaps, more accurately, it is important to ask not which questions are right or which are wrong, but rather which are relevant to the healthy and hopeful survival of humanity at this time – because, of course, some of the most destructive questions we have ever asked of one another concern what is right and what wrong. There is no time for such questions in this essay.

Time is an intrinsic element in the process of questioning. There has to be a certain sequential pattern in this type of discourse and a patience of application that does not preclude the persistence of inquiry. It therefore follows almost naturally to say that the Socratic method of question and answer is the kernel for the Western model of linear thinking. But there is something equally holistic in this model which lends itself to an interpretation more inclined towards Oriental philosophy. Questions themselves become a form of answer, and no answer is complete unless it carries the seeds of another question. The linear sense of time is conflated into a single moment that comprehends eternity. Both these traditions apply to the questions that occur to a student of Bahá'í thought. Both are relevant to all that follows.

I would like to evaluate questions in Bahá'í philosophy by looking briefly at selected episodes in Bahá'í history. We find, in even such a cursory study, the tradition of question-asking to be a deeply-rooted and time-honoured one. Those early 'God-intoxicated' heroes of the Bábí dispensation, many of whom were scholars, had prepared themselves for the advent of the Promised One and established what would constitute their measure of faith in Him by gathering questions which they wished Him to elucidate. It was due to specific questions asked that many of Bahá'u'lláh's Tablets were revealed, and in response to them that His addendum to His *Book of Laws* – *Questions and Answers* (*Su'ál va Javváb*) – was written after 1878. That well-known book compiled by Laura Clifford Barney, *Some Answered Questions*, is based on the precise questions asked by Western pilgrims who were seated at 'Abdu'l-Bahá's table in the House of 'Abdu'lláh Páshá between 1904 and 1906; and if one is frustrated by the questions missed, one knows it to be due to the interests of that group rather than the insight of 'Abdu'l-Bahá. The treasure house of correspondence, moreover, from Shoghi Effendi to many individuals and institutions around the world, inherited by the Universal House of Justice, evolved from the stream of questions addressed to him throughout the thirty-six years of his ministry, and the questions have not ceased any more than has the guidance.

No other religion has placed so subtle and significant a value on this method of exchange. The Jehovah of the Old Testament communicated to His chosen people on tablets of stone; the Ten Commandments provide no room for debate. Christ's parables brought more elasticity to the interchange between mankind and its Creator, but they too are self-contained; one gets nowhere with them using intellectual analysis or reasoning. Muḥammad wrote by dictation, under the pressure of persecution, and although the Qur'án is itself constructed on the model of question and answer, there was no chance in those rugged circumstances for leisured inquiry. When this principle was put into effect in the theological colleges, in the schools of priests and Islamic scholars, it was used to spawn a thousand divisions in the single point of knowledge and led to wars of blood as well as ink.

In the Bahá'í dispensation questions have not only reflected the mode of communication but also the philosophy underlying it. The stylistic pattern of question and answer frequently informs the structure of Bahá'u'lláh's Tablets. *The Tablet of Carmel*, for example, contains this pattern and the entire *Fire Tablet* is built upon it. There is frequently in His prayers and meditations a dialogue involving question and answer between 'the spirit of Bahá' and His Source, between the Pen and the Will of Him Who holds it. Often the questions far outnumber any answers and we are left with these haunting cries in our ears, questions destined to echo across the next thousand years:

> How long will ye persist in your waywardness? How long will ye refuse to reflect? How long ere ye shake off your slumber and are roused from your heedlessness? How long will ye remain unaware of the truth? . . . Pause for but a little while and reflect, O Minister, and be fair in thy judgement. What is it that We have committed that could justify thee in having slandered Us . . .? How, then, didst thou pronounce thy verdict against Me, when thou hadst not heard My testimony from Mine own lips?[5]

Questions have a powerful rhetorical impact and before we submit our judgement to their sway we need to distinguish between their different motivations and qualities. There are those which are rhetorical and belong to a specific literary tradition, and those which are entirely mystical and not intended to have any form of response. There is also a catechizing tradition of question and answer through which religious instruction is derived and it is useful to compare this tradition with what we find in Bahá'í history and notice the differences.

First of all, the rigidity of catechism is absent from the Bahá'í writings. There is no assumption, as the catechism requires, of set answers, of questions tailored towards a specific doctrinal response, from which the mind may not deviate. Secondly, there is a repetitive element in catechizing that aims to teach and learn by rote which is antithetical to the spirit of independent investigation in the Cause. Besides, as any student of catechism would endorse, it is the unspoken questions rather than those being asked which are the subject of real spiritual inquiry. Finally, the sheer multiplicity of questions one finds in even a cursory reading of *Prayers and Meditations*, for instance, suggests variety and diversity rather than repetition and dogmatism as a method of teaching. We also need to bear in mind that while the question may be the same, the answers may be tailored to the individual inquirer so that there might be different answers to the same question. As Bahá'u'lláh attests: 'Not everything that a man knoweth can be disclosed, nor can anything he can disclose be regarded as timely, nor can every timely utterance be considered as suited to the capacity of those who hear it.'[6]

In *The Dawn-Breakers* we find examples of false questions built upon a rhetoric of control, questions that do not actually want an answer, or rather, have a specific answer poised over the heads of the hearers. It is through such questions that mobs of people can be incited to violence, instigated and aroused to fanatical ends by the clergy.[7] These are examples of closed questions, catechizing questions, and it is significant that they are associated with priests and their power over people.

Some questions, we discover in *The Dawn-Breakers*,

were never asked, and had they been might have turned
the tide of history.[8] There are instances when a single
question can evoke volumes and other times when the
answer to a question is that there was no inquiry. In
response to a question from an individual believer about
the nature of that power, which according to Bahá'u'lláh
in *Epistle to the Son of the Wolf* might eliminate fear, Shoghi
Effendi wrote quite simply that since no one asked
Bahá'u'lláh to elucidate on the matter we cannot presume to guess what He meant by such a remark.[9] Sometimes too the petitioner fades and all trace of him is
forgotten except the response he has received. One of the
best-known and most often read Tablets of Bahá'u'lláh
which has been translated into English is addressed to a
man few may remember in any immediate or personal
sense, for the Aḥmad whose name is so often invoked in
the injunction to 'Learn well this Tablet' was a modest
and quiet man who simply obeyed that injunction
without achieving any outward significance.[10]

Other questions have survived in spite of having gone
almost too far. Mullá Ḥusayn, after being closely
questioned by the Báb about the instructions of Siyyid
Káẓim with regard to the distinguishing features of the
Promised One, is addressed by Him in these soul-
quaking words:

Behold, all these signs are manifest in Me![11]

The turmoil of uncertainty this unleashes in the breast of
the young seeker causes him to respond rather pre-
sumptuously and leaves him suffused with shame. He
has just determined on how he would respond should the
Báb raise this issue again when the latter, anticipating
his mental processes, rephrases the claim in the form of a

question: 'Observe attentively. Might not the Person intended by Siyyid Kázim be none other than I?'[12]

It is significant that Mullá Husayn's confusion first compels him to fall back on the list of questions he has compiled by which he is determined to test the validity of the Qá'im. Thus questions can also become a means of avoiding or delaying our encounters with truth. Maybe the nature of Mullá Husayn's questions at this time reflect that need for self-preservation, for he falls back upon erudition and scholarly analysis as a way of hedging his doubts. We might pause to ponder why the Báb rephrases His astounding claim as an interrogation rather than a statement and may be impressed in retrospect by the fact that He responds to the second question before He is asked; but we forget that the impact of this response would have been lost on a Mullá Husayn who had had no questions to ask in the first place. His soul has been prepared by this spirit of inquiry, a condition surely akin to that which we intend by the easy phrase 'independent investigation of truth' and equally as far from a tendency towards contentiousness and carping criticism. No doubt his presumption is forgiven because of this. Although he has tested God when it is for God to test His servants, there is in his motives a purity and an unquenchable thirst for truth which his questions, however clumsily, reflect. Like unwieldy vehicles they lumber out carrying their subtle load. How it makes one yearn to have refined the art of questioning when the finest motions of the soul can be contained by such a means!

Mullá Husayn appears to have refined his art by the time he is searching for the 'Treasure' concealed in Tihrán. When a stranger comes into his chamber at midnight overwhelmed by the significance of the conversation he has overheard, Mullá Ḥusayn probes his visitor with searching questions:

' "What is your name and which city is your home?"

' "My name," I replied, "is Mullá Muḥammad, and my surname Muʿallim. My home is Núr, in the province of Mázindarán."

' "Tell me," further inquired Mullá Ḥusayn, "is there today among the family of the late Mírzá Buzurg-i-Núrí, who was so renowned for his character, his charm, and artistic and intellectual achievements, anyone who has proved himself capable of maintaining the high traditions of that illustrious house?"

' "Yea," I replied, "among his sons now living, one has distinguished Himself by the very traits which characterized His father. By His virtuous life, His high attainments, His loving-kindness and liberality, He has proved Himself a noble descendant of a noble father." '

As the luminous presence of Bahá'u'lláh glimmers through these answers the pulse of the questioner begins to beat with a rising rhythm of excitement: 'What is His occupation?' 'What of His rank and position?' 'What is His name?' 'In which of the scripts of His father does He excel?' 'How does He spend His time?' 'What is His age?'[13]

Why, we might ask, is Mullá Ḥusayn concerned with the kind of script Bahá'u'lláh uses? There are of course precise contemporary answers to this question which will provide the substance of scholarly dissertations in comparative religion, calligraphy and linguistics for centuries to come but I am more interested in the value this question might have to those of us who are not scholars in any traditional sense, and for whom the word 'script' has no more subtle connotation than 'the chosen vehicle of communication for language'. It is fascinating that among his questions should be one probing the nature of Bahá'u'lláh's method of communication. All the subtle details of interaction between writer and reader, between question and answer, between concept and context, between meaning and interpretation are captured by this one symbolic question: 'In which of the scripts of His father does He excel?'

The irony here lies in the fact that the man who is providing Mullá Ḥusayn with answers becomes increasingly bewildered as he does so. Clearly not all answers are intended to remove doubts! But for Mullá Ḥusayn it seems that questions are his path to certitude; even when his face is radiant with it he does not cease from quiet persistence:

'Turning to me, with his face beaming with satisfaction and joy, he once more inquired . . .'[14] To the last moment of that nocturnal conversation we hear his questions still echoing, eager for more. Giving his midnight visitor a precious scroll wrapped in a piece of cloth with instructions that this should be delivered into the hands of Bahá'u'lláh at dawn, he finally asks, in parting: 'Should He deign to answer me, will you be kind enough to acquaint me with His reply?'[15]

Clearly these are different kinds of questions from those with which he approached the Báb; there are valleys of inquiry too one must needs traverse on this journey. But there are also just as many ways of crossing those valleys – and with a single step perhaps – that seem to depend less on the linear process of questions than on an instant comprehension which transcends answers too. There are those who lift their faces to us from the pages of *The Dawn-Breakers* with their questing souls so subtly fixed on their spiritual goal that the questions which rise like sea foam to their lips turn to vapour in the sun. The words they utter are mere outward sounds and symbols of a long inward communion in which question and answer have been rolled into one. The travel-stained and dishevelled youth who embraces Mullá Ḥusayn in the streets and asks if he has attained his goal can never be satisfied with the conventional formula of ordinary conversation, question and answer. Fixing his gaze on the receding figure of the Báb, he turns to the older man and says, simply, 'Why seek you to hide Him from me? I can recognize Him by His gait.' When Mullá Ḥusayn relates this mystery to the Báb, he is answered by another: 'Marvel not at his strange behaviour. We have in the world of the spirit been communing with that youth. We know him already. We indeed awaited his coming.'[16]

Quddús, that wonderful youth, is the embodiment of detachment from both questions and answers, a condition not easy to emulate in this contingent world. After recording this mysterious episode, Nabíl, the historian, immediately plunges into a paragraph replete with rhetorical questions of his own that are an attempt to fathom the mystery. Clearly the more mundane among us need to keep one foot at least in discursive prose if we are to follow these rare souls on their journeys.

The relationship between Mullá Ḥusayn and Quddús, the first and the last of the Letters of the Living, is similar, perhaps, to that of question and answer. Perhaps their response to the interrogation of this Revelation is also like an answer to a question. It might best be summed up in the words of another of these Letters, whose instantaneous acceptance of the Báb is couched in her poem:

> The effulgence of Thy face flashed forth,
> and the rays of Thy visage arose on high.
> Then speak the word, 'Am I not your Lord?'
> and 'Thou art, Thou art!' we will all reply.[17]

They belong to a generation who had accumulated centuries of questions, and who heard in the trumpet call of the Báb a challenge that only the Bugle of Bahá'u'lláh could adequately answer.

The last episode recorded by Nabíl about the strange interrelationship between the first and last Letters of the Living occurs at the moment of Mullá Ḥusayn's death. When he is carried, bleeding and unconscious, into the Fort at Shaykh Ṭabarsí, having been shot in the breast, Quddús requests that everyone should leave them alone together, explaining that 'There are certain confidential matters which I desire him alone to know.' A few moments later, according to the evidence of certain prying witnesses, and to their conjoined amazement, 'we heard the voice of Mullá Ḥusayn replying to questions from Quddús'. That Quddús should raise his fellow-believer from this unconscious state in order to inform him of 'confidential matters' is strange enough, but that he temporarily suspends the moment of his friend's death in order to ask him questions is more wonderful still.

The question and answer period continues for two hours, and Mullá Ḥusayn, glimpsed by those same eavesdroppers 'through a fissure in the door', is seen to have arisen from his couch and seated himself in his customary manner, on bended knees, beside Quddús; and with bowed head and downcast eyes, is apparently

listening intently to every word and answering the
latter's questions. Strangest and most wonderful are the
last words we hear, our ears pressed against the door of
the past, when Mullá Ḥusayn says to Quddús, 'Are you
well pleased with me?'

A great mystery lingers in the silence that ensues and
in the fact that it was earlier probed. This last
interrogation held like a brimming cup to the very lips
of death symbolizes a degree of comprehension un-
matched by anything Mullá Ḥusayn may have known
before. 'Things which previously I deemed it unallowable
to utter', relays Quddús, 'I have now shared with him.'[18]
The faint smile lingering at his lips, the utter tranquillity
of his countenance which indicate sleep rather than
death, all serve to confirm our hesitant guess that
whatever the nature of those questions, and indeed
however Quddús may have chosen to answer that last
poignant request, these were the means of enveloping a
heroic soul in what may only be described, prosaically,
as bliss.

Questions clearly have a privileged role to play in Bahá'í
thought. Besides being employed to penetrate the very
soul of man, they have been welcomed, given courteous
consideration, and patiently answered by the central
figures of our Faith.

'Ask Me whatsoever you please,' said the Báb to one
whose vacillations and fear led finally to his inability to
bear the consequences of his own questions. 'Set forth
whatsoever perplexes your mind, and I will, by the aid of
God, unloose My tongue and undertake to resolve your
problems . . .'[19]

On a later occasion in the city of Iṣfáhán before 'an

assemblage of the most brilliant and accomplished divines' of that city, the Báb is requested by the Mu'tamid to expound the nature and demonstrate the validity of Muḥammad's 'Specific Mission', to which He instantly rejoins:

'Which do you prefer, a verbal or a written answer to your question?'

'A written reply,' he answered, 'not only would please those who are present at this meeting, but would edify and instruct both present and future generations.'[20]

We have to thank the Mu'tamid for his far-sighted response; the principle he articulates here is one on which a large body of Bahá'í writings is based. Furthermore the manner in which he responds to the Báb's question does him honour too, before both present and future generations.

Sometimes in early Bahá'í history we find, however, that those who ask questions or respond to them demonstrate their narrow-mindedness with glaring self-ignorance. It needs no prolixity to establish a fool. When the Báb is being examined at Tabríz, for instance, before a roomful of learned Islamic scholars, He is interrupted in His first invocation by someone who protests against an 'infraction of the rules of grammar'. Proceeding once more with His invocation, He is again interrupted by a second interlocutor who, to his unmitigated shame before the scorn of future historians, asks, 'To which tense does the word Ishtartanna belong?'[21] No doubt there are certain questions which will continue to embarrass us beyond the grave. Questions are indeed of an opacity at times that they not only penetrate the subject being probed by inquiry but the inquirer too. Such questions condemn the questioner.

Against examples like these where arrogance betrays a shallowness of character and obscurantist tendencies, we find figures such as Siyyid Yaḥyá, later named Vaḥíd, whose questions serve to enhance rather than hamper a comprehension of truth.[22] The Siyyid's learning and erudition recommend him to Muḥammad Sháh as a fit ambassador to 'inquire thoroughly into the episode of the Siyyid-i-Báb', and he sets out for Shíráz to investigate the matter as much on his own behalf as on that of his sovereign. 'On his way,' Nabíl informs us, 'he conceived the various questions which he thought he would submit to the Báb. Upon the replies which the latter gave to these questions would, in his view, depend the truth and validity of His mission.' Thus he proceeds on his first interview to direct the Báb's attention 'to the most abstruse and bewildering themes in the metaphysical teachings of Islám, to the obscurest passages of the Qur'án, and to the mysterious traditions and prophecies of the imáms of the Faith.'

The Báb's response is fascinating. First He listens with the utmost courtesy and respect, then He notes the questions and begins to give a brief reply to each one. It is not His erudition nor subtlety of argument, nor indeed the abstruse and obscure nature of His comments that thrill Siyyid-i-Yaḥyá to admiration but, conversely, their 'conciseness and lucidity'. This is all the more remarkable since, unlike so many of his contemporaries, he is not offended by such answers. He is not so attached to his own questions that their intellectual virtuosity blinds him. On the contrary, these questions, viewed from the lucid perspective of the Báb's few words, strike him as horribly stuffed with self-importance. 'I have in His presence', he confesses afterwards, 'expatiated unduly upon my own learning.' In other words, the Báb's answers cause him to question himself.

More fascinating still, during the course of his second interview, he finds quite unaccountably 'that all the questions which he had intended to submit to the Báb had vanished from his memory', but that to his great surprise, 'the Báb was answering, with the same lucidity and conciseness that had characterized His previous replies, those same questions which he had momentarily forgotten'. What are we to make of this interesting conundrum? His questions, so laboriously constructed, are clearly irrelevant since he can so rapidly forget them. Yet without them how would Vaḥíd have been able to measure the unfathomable significance of what the Báb was doing? However puny and wordy they might be before the vast and silent immensity of God, they are nevertheless necessary markers to chart the unknown territories of the soul. Vaḥíd records that he felt as though he were locked fast in a trance-like sleep but that the words of the Báb, 'His answers to questions which I had forgotten to ask, reawakened me'.

The interrogation, at this point, becomes an inward one. Doubting himself and the experience of his senses, as well as the sanity of his mind, Vaḥíd begs leave to retire in order to regain possession of his faculties and conceal the agitation he is in. He determines on a conclusive test for his last interview with the Báb, at which he might decide, once and for all, whether His claims were to be trusted. I quote his own words, as recorded by Nabíl:

I resolved that in my third interview with the Báb I would in my inmost heart request Him to reveal for me a commentary on the Súrih of Kaw<u>th</u>ar. I determined not to breathe that request in His presence. Should He, unasked by me, reveal this commentary in a manner that would immediately distinguish it in my eyes from the prevailing standards current among the commentators on the Qur'án, I then would be convinced of the Divine character of His Mission . . .

What ensues has about it the nature of a dream, and certainly there are many questions that one would have liked to have asked Vaḥíd and that remain, almost a century later, still reverberating in our minds. Would psychoanalysis be appropriate here? Can we impute hypnotism to the Báb? How well prepared was Vaḥíd, after all, if he can be so overpowered by stage fright? Is it something more than stage fright? What exactly did he see in the face of the Báb, which has been frequently described, and by impartial observers, to be one of the most gentle of countenances, which could have affected him in this unnerving way?

As soon as I was ushered into His presence, a sense of fear, for which I could not account, suddenly seized me. My limbs quivered as I beheld His face. I, who on repeated occasions had been introduced into the presence of the <u>Sh</u>áh and had never discovered the slightest trace of timidity in myself, was now so awed and shaken that I could not remain standing on my feet.

The Báb, aware of his plight, rises and takes him by the hand to conduct him to a seat beside Him. Even now, at this moment of acute stress, His comment relates directly to Vaḥíd's desire to question Him: 'Seek from Me', He says, 'whatever is your heart's desire. I will

readily reveal it to you.' Maybe it is this very invitation
to ask more questions that is Vahíd's final undoing: the
good Siyyid is past questioning. He has been reduced to
the condition of 'a babe that can neither understand nor
speak'. What are we to make of this? Must all our
questions strive then to this goal of self-immolation?
Must we yearn towards a knowledge that will deprive us
of speech, leave us spellbound in our unknowing? The
Báb gazes at him, smiling, and delivers the final
thunderbolt:

> Were I to reveal for you the commentary on the Súrih
> of Kawthar, would you acknowledge that My words
> are born of the Spirit of God? Would you recognize
> that My utterance can in no wise be associated with
> sorcery or magic?

These are the questions, finally, and not Vahíd's,
which survive the passage of time and cause us to
ponder. What, after all, is the point of an answer if it will
only confirm us in our superstitions? What even is the
value of divining the question if that in itself were not an
adequate answer for us? The Báb responds to Vahíd's
questions with His own, which are simply stated and
perfectly lucid. Oh, but how they give us pause to
wonder on matters more abstruse and equally obtuse as
any delivered by a pompous scholar!

Later in Nabíl's chronicle when we read the circumstances of Vahíd's martyrdom we hear from his own lips
an account of this memorable event. It is significant to
note that this was an experience thrust upon him and not
personally chosen, for as he says, the late Muḥammad
Sháh

> . . . asked me to report personally to him the results of

my inquiry, inasmuch as I was the only one among the ecclesiastical leaders of Ṭihrán in whom he could repose implicit confidence. I undertook that mission with the firm resolution of confuting the arguments of that siyyid, of inducing Him to abandon His ideas and to acknowledge my leadership, and of conducting Him with me to Ṭihrán as a witness to the triumph I was to achieve.

His pomposity as the chosen agent of Muḥammad Sháh combines with the instinctive pride of the scholar who feels himself to be master of his subject. It is a lethal combination guaranteed to leave no room whatsoever in the mind for the possibility of unasked questions. Yet there is clearly some other element in Vaḥíd's nature that has made him susceptible to the experience that follows:

> When I came into His presence, however, and heard His words, the opposite of that which I had imagined took place. In the course of my first audience with Him, I was utterly abashed and confounded; by the end of the second, I felt as helpless and ignorant as a child; the third found me as lowly as the dust beneath His feet.[23]

The magnanimity of God, however, exceeds the obtuseness of pedants as well as the pride of politicians. As Nabíl tells the story, it is still early in the afternoon when the Báb calls for His pen-case and some paper, and proceeds to fulfil Vaḥíd's unspoken request. He does not lay down His pen until sunset and during the interim He writes ceaselessly in conjunction with the sweet murmur of His chanting voice. When the commentary is complete He reads it aloud to the unspeakable joy of the dazed

Siyyid and then rises to depart. It takes Vaḥíd and Mullá 'Abdu'l-Karím three days and three nights to complete a transcription of this work, verifying all the traditions in the text as they do so and discovering, to their amazement, all to be entirely accurate. 'Such was the state of certitude', Vaḥíd concludes, 'to which I had attained that if all the powers of the earth were to be leagued against me they would be powerless to shake my confidence in the greatness of His Cause.'[24]

Many of the deepest questions in the Bahá'í teachings, like Vaḥíd's request, are answered by more questions, which in turn carry us towards that most vibrant state known as certitude.

Thus if we wish to think about the implications of any one of the laws of Bahá'u'lláh – the laws pertaining to fasting, for example, and the obligatory laws, with their attendant exemptions, the laws of inheritance and the Ḥuqúqu'lláh – we will find ourselves, in turn, asking more questions about the nature of justice, the purpose of law, the symbolism of word and deed, the relationship between all these and that ambiguous word 'equality'. And if we turn to history for evidence and 'truth', we find such inquiries must necessarily lead us to ask questions about the motives of historians, ourselves included, the justice and method of the selection of facts, the philosophy underlying our own and others' inquiries, to say nothing of how all the above influence our evidence of contemporary events. And again, if we are to pursue some of the so-called 'principles' of Bahá'í thought in order to pin them down to practical application we cannot do so without spawning a thousand more questions which will send us scurrying into apparently unrelated areas of concern. So, for example, we might find that exhortations from the pen of Bahá'u'lláh directed to some of the notorious tyrants of His day may well seem congruent to matters concerning family life, and reflections upon the imagery of His most mystical writings might illumine our understanding of sexual equality.

Such questions demand a discriminating courage which is akin to that characterized by some of the Dawn-Breakers of this Faith. And it is therefore with the spirit of inquiry shared by Vaḥíd and by Mullá Ḥusayn, by the clear-browed Quddús and by Ṭáhirih, who was prepared in advance to recognize answers since she had been so early trained by her father to ask questions, that I embark on these essays. I take confidence in the fact that Bahá'u'lláh so many times enjoins us to 'ponder', to 'consider', to 'call to mind', all of which, baldly enough, mean think. And one way to think, certainly, is to question oneself, and the writings, and everything else one can read, and all that one might experience. I take confidence too in that Bahá'u'lláh often anticipates such questions, encourages them: 'And now regarding thy question . . .' He begins, and again, 'And now concerning thy question . . .'

The breadth of His response, the generosity of His replies is just one of the many meanings inherent in that exquisite image, 'The Book of God is wide open, and His Word is summoning mankind unto Him.'[25] Were our questions, leaping up from just as open hearts, to reflect even in a small measure such immense generosity, how much might unfold before us indeed! It is only when we fear the question or anticipate too narrowly an answer that we condemn ourselves to stunted growth and inflict such great dishonour on ourselves and on this Cause by imagining that its purpose is to bring us a mere code of

replies. In this attitude lies the danger of fundamentalism. When Bahá'u'lláh asserts that His very laws are like
the choice wine that is at last unsealed, how can we
impute anything less magnanimous to His entire purpose?
If this Revelation does not cause the individual mind and
spirit to stretch out its limbs and search for the measure
of its freedom, how can it carry forward a civilization,
leave alone advance it? With searching questions,
therefore, and in a spirit of humility, with courageous
questions that topple our preconceived notions and erect
in their stead structures which aspire beyond any ready
answers, might we approach this mysterious Cause.

2

About Scholarship

One of the questions I would like to raise concerns the meaning of scholarship in the Bahá'í Faith. Since scholarship has an ancient tradition of its own and the Bahá'í Faith has a forward-looking vision, the link between the two may serve to illustrate Bahá'u'lláh's revolutionary harmony, may provide an example of how the past and the future, like so many apparent contraries, lie along one continuum according to Bahá'í philosophy. Frequently we discover that the patterns of behaviour containing a specific set of symbolic values in an earlier society change both in structure and value with the introduction of a new religious impulse, but all these changes, these reversals and transpositions only emerge as a result of process and the message they convey is one of process.

Christ's principle of 'loving one's neighbour' enshrined in the parable of the Good Samaritan, and Bahá'u'lláh's principle of 'unity in diversity' emphasized repeatedly throughout His writings, show us a process of development in human relationships. We cannot leap from one to the other, abandoning the first or assuming the second to be 'superior' in any moral sense. The moral values implicit in both precepts are identical, but what has changed is the scope of application. The difference draws our attention to process. Similarly, early religious rituals involving human sacrifice for the appeasement of the gods became translated in Judeo-Christian terms to a sacrifice of divine proportions that might, if properly understood, elevate the station of mankind. And by the time we read, in Bahá'u'lláh's *Hidden Words*, 'write with that crimson ink that hath been shed in My path'[1] all these associations are linked and amplified as we move from physical martyrdom to the concept of sacrifice, and finally arrive at the mysterious involvement implied in this present stage of our development: 'Write all that We have revealed unto thee with the ink of light upon the tablet of thy spirit.'[2] It is the *process* involved about which we learn here and not a value judgement based on false comparisons.

I would like to glance at what has happened to scholarship as a process and to see what its implications might be, in Bahá'í terms, for the future, based on its roots in the past. In order to do this I would like first to emphasize the link between priests and scholars in most religious traditions that I have encountered so that we can better evaluate the inheritance bequeathed to the institution of scholarship today.

The fundamental purpose of scholarship in early religious societies was closely linked to the institution of priesthood. It was the role of the scholar, that keeper of the Word, to elucidate on matters that the priest, that interpreter of the Word, might teach the multitude. Moreover, in Judaism, Christianity and Islám there has evolved a mass of written material in addition to the Word, scribbled by generations of scholars and priests, material consisting of commentary and history, extraneous tradition and jurisprudence, all of which serves to bolster, buttress and very often blind the impact of the

Word itself. In societies where the masses were illiterate and secular government was largely authoritarian and, for the most part, male-dominated, it was inevitable that a parallel institution, with a similar hierarchical structure, should exist by which spiritual authority could be administered. In fact it is more than likely that secular governance developed upon the patterns already set by spiritual authority and that temporal leaders could only with considerable struggle find autonomy from the paternalistic control of priests. Not every Arthur had a wise Merlin at his side. Scholarship and priestcraft, therefore, were alternative expressions for, and at one time dominant forms of, man's desire for power.

With this brief historical perspective in mind, it is illuminating to turn to the pages of Bahá'í history and notice that from the outset the Bahá'í Revelation has been associated with scholars. Whilst Christ's earliest disciples were fishermen, those of the Báb were threadbare students of the Qur'án; while the followers of Muḥammad rose with the sword to vindicate His holy name, the exemplars of the Bábí Revelation dipped their reed pens into ink with the same fervour. Ṭáhirih writing her eloquent proofs in captivity, Quddús reading his commentaries as the cannon balls roll at his feet, and Nabíl immortalizing both their lives in his chronicles all bear witness to the close association between the passion inspired by this Cause and the patient diligence of a mind seeking after truth. Many previous Manifestations have caused the halt to walk and the lame to run, the blind to see and the dead to rise again; in the religious history of this Faith we find in addition that illiterate souls become lucid philosophers, merchants and tradesmen are erudite scholars and sifters of wheat turn to metaphysics.

It is equally illuminating, however, to notice that from
the outset this Faith has been profoundly anti-clerical.
Some of its most eloquent advocates, trained for priesthood, turned aside from their calling; some of its most
passionate adherents, questioning this very training,
used their schools and madrisihs to proclaim the new
Cause they had espoused. Small wonder then that the
priests, the mullás and mujtahids of Shí'ih Islám have
remained among the fiercest and most ruthless enemies
of the Bahá'í Faith.

The greatest challenge to this generation of Bahá'ís,
and one of the first questions raised by those who eagerly
turn to this Faith, searching for evidence of hope, rests in
this enigmatic relationship between scholars and priests.
We say we have no priesthood; why then the emphasis
on scholarship? How can we purge the scholar of that old
power-hungry desire to interpret the Word? How can we
ensure that we are not merely creating a kind of
'priestcraft' under the guise of 'Bahá'í scholarship'?
When we recall the story of Vahíd, his education through
questions at the hands of the Báb, his fervent detachment
from his own scholarship as the truth of the Báb's Cause
dawns upon him, we must not forget that remarkable
episode recorded by 'Abdu'l-Bahá in *Memorials of the
Faithful* in which He remembers sitting on the lap of
Táhirih as she listened, silent and veiled, to the eloquent
excitement of Vahíd.[3] He was enumerating, as men of his
profession are wont to do, and no doubt with a degree of
detail and precision characteristic of scholars, all the
'signs and verses that bore witness to the advent of the
new Manifestation'. Interrupting his enthusiastic catalogue with pre-emptory impatience, she reminds him
that this is a time for deeds and not words, that if he is 'a

man of true learning' he should demonstrate his faith by action and not merely by analysis. 'Cease idly repeating the traditions of the past,' she vehemently declares, '. . . and rend asunder the veils of idle fancy.' It is an astonishing statement, uttered fearlessly beneath the roof of Bahá'u'lláh with the symbol of His Covenant seated upon her lap. If we were looking for Bahá'í iconography, here may we find its beginnings!

This response, so rich with symbolism, is not only characteristic of Ṭáhirih, but somehow significant to the present study. We need to question in this same spirit the purpose of scholarship, the contrast between deeds and words, and the value of any veils, including the intellectual ones.

In order to explore some of these questions and excavate a few more I would like to turn first to the story, from *The Dawn-Breakers*, of a man who chose scholarship as his profession, who became a dedicated student of Islamic law in order to seek for what he called 'the mystery of God'.[4] Having reached the decision at 'the age of maturity' that this was a mystery worth pursuing, Mullá 'Abdu'l-Karím realized that 'nothing short of the acquisition of learning . . . could enable me to achieve my goal'. But when he begins to tell of the adventures to which this led him, he abjures the language of learning for a much more ancient tongue. His exposition has nothing of the detached tones of an objective scholar and uses a formula more familiar to poets than academics. 'Hear me,' he says, '[and] I will relate to you the tale of a strange experience, a tale which I have shared with no one until now.'

The teller of tales has always commanded attention. In fact, the power of religion has from ancient times always resided with those who could tell 'the best of stories' in such a way as to mesmerize listeners. Besides, the hint of secrecy combined with the narrative style is irresistible. Mírzá Muḥammad-'Alí and his brother, who are Mullá 'Abdu'l-Karím's listeners, are riveted. Had he embarked upon a solemn disquisition, painstakingly pruned of all personal reference, they and we and future generations would no doubt have soon been yawning; for what he introduces us to is the preoccupation and habits of a typical Islamic scholar, hardly a subject of great fascination. 'Study and research' are his life. He methodically applies himself to 'every available branch of human learning', after two years of which he resolves 'to master the intricacies of Muslim jurisprudence and theology'. He is well on the way to becoming a member of what Roy Mottahedeh calls 'this charmed circle' which was also 'a closed circle . . . whose members, in their arrogant pride in their largely useless learning, deluded themselves into thinking that they had something useful to say about the urgent tasks of the time'.[5] His life shrinks within the confines of 'a room in one of the madrisihs of Qazvín', his contact with the outside world is limited to discussions with his fellow disciples. Just the mere catalogue of his thoroughness is enough to merit yawns, but we are alert, aware that something unexpected might occur, as it usually does in a story, in the middle of an ordinary day.

When his diligence finally reaps its own rewards and he 'graduates', so to speak, one of the most outstanding divines of Qazvín elevates his rank to that of a mujtahid and offers to make, after the congregational prayer on the following Friday, a public announcement of his prowess as a scholar and a priest. Naturally, this is an honour calling for extensive celebration, but it is here that our story-telling expectations are fulfilled and Mullá 'Abdu'l-Karím's tale becomes both unusual and interesting. He requests that his family delay the celebrations and retires once more to his solitary, scholastic cell, 'pondering', as he puts it, 'the following thoughts in my heart'.

Years of mental discipline now bear their fruit. What he does at this point is to bring the full force of his careful and meticulous mind, the analytical probing of his thoughts, and all the trim and tackle of his training to bear upon the validity of his present position. He questions his true deserts. He questions the purity of his motives. Beneath the arc light of this scrutiny he questions everything, even the role of the priest towards which he had aspired.

> Had you not fondly imagined, I said to myself, that only the sanctified in spirit could ever hope to attain the station of an authoritative expounder of the sacred Scriptures of Islám? Was it not your belief that whoso attained this station would be immune from error? . . . Be fair. Do you in your own heart regard yourself as having attained that state of purity and sublime detachment . . . Think you yourself to be free from every taint of selfish desire? . . . Your aim in acquiring all this learning, I thought to myself, has been to unravel the mystery of God and to attain the state of certitude. Be fair. Are you sure of your own interpretation of the Qur'án? Are you certain that the laws which you promulgate reflect the will of God?

After a sleepless night, a night during whose darkest hours he has to admit that 'the rust of learning had corroded my soul and obscured my vision', these searing questions turn to yearning prayers and he lifts his thoughts away from his limitations and towards his God. 'I am lost in bewilderment', he confesses, 'at the thought of the multitude of sects into which Thy holy Faith hath fallen. I am deeply perplexed when I behold the schisms that have torn the religions of the past. Wilt Thou guide me in my perplexities, and relieve me of my doubts?' In the midst of these unanswerable appeals he loses consciousness and has a strange dream.

The dream, like the lyrical beginning of his mysterious tale, lifts him and his listeners out of one set of expectations into another, from one level of inquiry into another. In it he sees a teacher towards whom he advances, and waking he knows he has yet more to learn. It is not that his questions are answered but rather that he can pursue them with renewed vigour and follow them to unpremeditated ends. As a result of this dream he turns aside from his career, forgoes his honours, excuses himself from his old teacher and directs his steps immediately to Karbilá, where he has learnt there resides one Siyyid Kázim-i-Rashtí, the forerunner of the Báb.

Although he leaves the shores of traditional scholarship, he embarks on a new stage of education in which he applies all the training and discipline he has received to the theme that constitutes 'the sole subject' of his new teacher's classes: the manifestation and imminent appearance of the Promised Qá'im. Every logical proposition, every philosophical premise on which he has exercised his mind is now bent to explore this end. No matter what the verse or tradition under discussion, Siyyid Kázim invariably relates it to this theme, urging his students to prepare themselves, to purify their souls and ponder on the importance of recognizing One

Whom, as he stressed, 'lives in the midst of this people'.

Ironically, it is in order to take up a profession that is similarly obscure and 'in the midst of people' that Mullá 'Abdu'l-Karím finally returns to the city of Qazvín to be a simple merchant. He dreads this return. He knows it will provoke the ire of the mullás who naturally felt the sting of his refusal to join their ranks. But following the advice of his teacher and ignoring entirely 'their machinations', he quietly assumes the role of an ordinary tradesman, transacts his business by day and continues his soul-searching by night. 'With tearful eyes', he recalls, 'I would commune with God.' And it is during these meditations, one evening, when he is 'so wrapt in prayer that [he] seemed to have fallen into a trance' that he has his second dream.

This time the dream is even more mysterious. Reading it we realize that we have left the objective world of scholarship far behind and the world of story-telling as well. Unlike the first invitation to sit back and simply listen, or the second to arise and seek out one who would answer our dilemmas, the experience of this vision questions the dreamer and the reader alike. Instead of seeing a man who offers guidance, as he does in his first dream, 'Abdu'l-Karím discovers a bird, white-plumed as new fallen snow, hovering above his head. It alights on a tree beside him and ushers both him and us into a mystical world, a world where questions transcend egress and regress, where they simply hover, filled with their own potentialities:

Are you seeking the Manifestation, O 'Abdu'l-Karím?

The bird, it seems, has spoken to him 'in accents of indescribable sweetness.' The question reverberates above him and then concludes with this curious answer, 'Lo, the year '60.' Whereupon he wakes.

The experience agitates 'Abdu'l-Karím unbearably. All his years of patient scholarship, all his painstaking training, all his detachment from worldly recognition, his abdication from power, his acquiescence, have not cost him as much turmoil of spirit as does this strange question and its enigmatic answer. His first dream, while it caused him to alter radically the paths of his career, was nevertheless a dream which a young scholar might find familiar; he remained on home territory within its context. Its challenge was traditional. But this dream is unnerving. It comes to him from worlds beyond the madrisih or even the marketplace. He is obsessed by the mystery of the few brief words he hears. He is haunted by the memory and beauty of the vision. And in his wonder he 'revolved it constantly in my mind . . . shared it with no one, fearing lest its sweetness forsake me'.

Secrecy has enthralled us once more, but even as it does so we realize he has at that very moment broken his silence. Even as we savour the mystery, we know his words have been reported by Mírzá Muḥammad and his brother to Nabíl, who has in turn recorded them for Bahá'u'lláh, and for all the subsequent readers of *The Dawn-Breakers*. The fact is that the moment of his telling coincides with the greatest of all the mysterious experiences of his life. No longer in either a dream or a trance, he finds himself, in the year '60 (1844), in the city of Kirmán, in the presence of the Báb. And there, in the company of others, including those to whom he is now explaining these curious circumstances, he finds that the Báb is turning to him and speaking 'with calm and extreme gentleness'. The words He utters take no profound scholarship to decipher. They are, precisely, the words of his dream.

' 'Abdu'l-Karím,' comes the soft atom-splitting interrogation, 'are you seeking the Manifestation?'

Among the many reasons why I think this episode vital to any discussion about the nature of scholarship is the simple fact that its conclusion defies analysis. That seems to me to be one of the prerequisites of a Bahá'í definition of scholarship: that we should admit, from the outset, the limitations of our analytical means and recognize the immensity that we leave unprobed by the scurryings of our minds. With that vast immensity unfathomed, the value and importance of scholarship can then assume its proper place, serving as it does as the foundation and not as the ultimate goal of 'Abdu'l-Karím's original motive.

The second fascinating element in this story is that the good Mullá has used his scholarship first and foremost to acquaint himself with the nature of his own motives and limitations. He is not deluded by his knowledge because it has merely served to highlight his lack of wisdom. 'I recognized myself', he records, 'as still a victim of cares and perplexities, of temptations and doubts.' While the aim of all learning may well be the knowledge of God, what the Mullá's story reminds us is that it would all have been a waste of time if this goal had been attempted by one whose days had been spent in utter ignorance of his true self.

The third interesting characteristic of 'Abdu'l-Karím's years of scholastic training is that it appears to have instilled in him a genuine humility, a disinclination to turn around, with these qualifications, and presume to tell others what to think. For all his accomplishments he does not feel he has any prerogative over truth, nor any right to dictate his interpretations of it to others. 'I was oppressed,' he says, 'by such thoughts as to how I should conduct my classes, how to lead my congregation in prayer, how to enforce the laws and precepts of the Faith.' He abjures the position of the priest even as he attains the goal of the scholar, which is to be one. Most revealing is his reason for doing this. To accept the role of the priest and his assumption of duties in a community, he admits, would be to accept the consequent enslavement to competition, arrogance and pedantry that attended such duties, an enslavement that constituted, for him, the very heart of loss. 'I felt continually anxious as to how I should discharge my duties, how to ensure the superiority of my achievements over those who had preceded me.' He achieves the true garland of his scholastic labours and becomes 'a fruit upon the tree of humility'[6] when he confesses in the dark night of his soul that 'the consciousness of error suddenly dawned upon me'.[7]

As the spokesman of a new day of consciousness, as a scholar redefined in the light of that new day, 'Abdu'l-Karím effectively alienates himself from all the old-world scholars. So profoundly insecure are the mullás of Qazvín that the abdication of one of their number causes 'protestations' and 'machinations'. It is a lesson not only in honesty and humility, therefore, but in profound courage that he teaches us by returning to Qazvín in the guise of a simple merchant. It is to such courage that Bahá'í scholars are summoned, a courage of disregarding that traditional academic over-anxiety to be accepted by one's peers. With such courage and without crude protestation, it might be possible to reverse quietly all the basic assumptions of an academic profession, its anxiety for prestige, its insecure and vicarious hunger for power, its preoccupation with 'making a mark' in whatever field. The sheer anonymity of this gentle scholar is one of the most threatening aspects of his behaviour.

Finally, and most significantly, the tale of Mullá 'Abdu'l-Karím tells us of scholarship because it is a tale and not a treatise, a story and not a theory, a piece of vivid narrative prose. That creativity is an essential characteristic of Bahá'í scholarship seems to be implied by Bahá'u'lláh's comment in the *Lawḥ-i-Ḥikmat* when He cautions His followers lest they 'despise the merits of My learned servants whom God hath graciously chosen to be the exponents of His Name "the Fashioner" amidst mankind.'[8] The word 'fashioner' and the exhortation immediately following that we 'develop such crafts and undertakings that everyone . . . may benefit therefrom' suggest a revolution in the definition of scholarship which is mirrored in the movement of Mullá 'Abdu'l-Karím's life from the cell to the marketplace. With its cyclical and beautifully constructed form, this tale conveys its theme of intellectual search through a literary style that seeks continually for practical expression. It is precisely this purpose which the dreams and visions serve, enhancing the mundane details of a life in a language at once poetic and mysterious. It is towards this purpose that the discourse of scholarship is surely leading him; for his final experience in the presence of the Báb, when he pales at that strange and haunting interrogation, bursts into tears and falls at the feet of His recognized Beloved, is not a condition that can be accurately commanded in the language of objective prose although it must profoundly change, from that very moment, the fabric of his daily life.

Mysteries are valued in this religion; they are not fabricated to keep us in awe but revered in order that we might question our glib assumptions. The language of proofs is richly twined in a counterpoint of poetry. There is not only a harmony between the two voices but a sense of continuity too, the kind of continuity that describes process. Proofs lead towards poetry, and poetry tends towards mysticism. And when it arrives at those farthest shores it sinks into silence. '. . . the mystery of this utterance is hid . . .' writes Bahá'u'lláh in *The Four Valleys*. 'It is sanctified above the jewels of explanation; it is beyond what the most subtle of tongues can tell.'[9] In the *Lawh-i-Ḥikmat*, He writes, 'When the discourse reached this stage, the dawn of divine mysteries appeared and the light of utterance was quenched.'[10]

That silence can be the strongest proof was made a spiritual commonplace by Christ whose only response to Pontius Pilate was 'Thou hast said.' No more. It is a proof, however, that is unappealing to scholars, who, as Bahá'u'lláh frequently points out, favour prolixity. When Bahá'u'lláh concludes that 'What I had written ere this hath been eaten by the flies, so sweet was the ink',[11] we are reminded of the quality of proof that needs no words, that resides in speechless comprehension, like love, that frequently finds itself explored in *The Dawn-Breakers* through episodes such as the final meeting between the Báb and Mullá 'Abdu'l-Karím, or through experiences such as that recorded by Qahru'lláh, the dervish from India.[12]

'In the days when I occupied the exalted position of a navváb in India,' he tells us, 'the Báb appeared to me in a vision. He gazed at me and won my heart completely. I arose and . . . started to follow Him . . .'

It is a strange and unnerving story, replete with enigmas, resonant with ambiguities, a fitting way, because so unsatisfying, to end these thoughts on scholarship, since scholarship is one of the ways the human mind seeks to control the unknown. The Indian navváb is commanded by the Báb in his vision to divest himself of all his gay apparel, dress himself in the clothes of a wandering dervish and seek out the Manifestation in the fortress fastness of Chihríq. He proceeds to walk all the way from his country to that forsaken place and once there attains his heart's desire. But his zeal provokes such an uproar in the vicinity of the prison that due to the turmoil he himself raises among the Kurdish leaders in Chihríq, orders are issued from the capital to transfer the Báb shortly thereafter to Tabríz.

Even as he attains his goal, therefore, he loses it. There are many questions that scholars may similarly pursue into the wilderness of silence, losing themselves and others in the process. Rising like a proverbial genie out of the great spaces of search with his tumultuous love he is finally commanded by the Báb to return 'alone and on foot . . . to his native land.' His obedience is as absolute as is his love. When he is offered assistance or companionship on that journey, Nabíl tells us, he refuses it. Clearly there are silences and mysteries in ourselves and others that may not be shared, silences of confession and shame, for instance, as well as silences of inexpressible aspiration and the most delicate of loves. To attempt to probe such places is to dabble in 'priestcraft'. It is enough for the dervish that he has known his Beloved, and that his Beloved knows him. He needs no priest and no one's words can adequately interpret what remains of his story.

The compelling force of his reply silenced those who begged to be allowed to journey with him. He refused to accept either money or clothing from anyone. Alone, clad in the meanest attire, staff in hand he walked all the way back to his country. No one knows what ultimately befell him.

3

Priestcraft

Once we begin to ask questions we become scholars, of sorts, and as soon as we think of ourselves as scholars we are in danger of acting like priests. What is it then in priestcraft that is so antithetical to the message and philosophy of the Bahá'í Faith? What principles underlie the fact that we have no clergy in this religion? Can we purge our psyches of the need for a priesthood just because it has been abrogated as an institution? Or are we in danger, irreligious as our society is, of turning lawyers and psychiatrists into priests, and assuming the mantle ourselves, even in the act of writing? Maybe the way to begin probing these questions is to consider the relationship of priesthood and power, and then to define what Shoghi Effendi means by 'priestcraft', which could be applied to the icons of a materialistic society as well as to the liturgy of a church or the tautology of a writer.

The word 'priestcraft' reveals more about those subject to its sway than those who command them. It suggests a certain weakness in human nature, a neediness, a tendency to look for leadership, a vulnerability that can be manipulated and abused. There have been many priests who did not commit the sacrilege to human dignity of wielding priestcraft, and there continue to be many people undistinguished by any cloth who employ it in the name of the law and medicine, education and art.

Priestcraft, it would seem, is the last relic of our superstitious fear of the unknown.

When we discover among the various prohibitions in Bahá'u'lláh's *Kitáb-i-Aqdas* one regarding priesthood, we need to set it in relation to several others which when linked together might be seen as being what Shoghi Effendi means by 'priestcraft'. Laws prohibiting asceticism, monasticism, the confession of sins and the use of pulpits and congregational prayer, even the muttering of sacred verses in the street and mendicancy, all seem to tend towards the same goal: that of demystifying the path of holiness, of democratizing the goal of the saint, of removing the clutter of self-appointed intermediaries between the soul and its Creator in the private act of prayer, and replacing the role of spiritual leader in the community with the common exhortation to all alike to become servants before God.

The most distinctive feature of this Revelation, however, and one which bears directly upon the warning against 'priestcraft' as well as the prohibition of priesthood, is the unequivocal nature of Bahá'u'lláh's Covenant, established in His Will and Testament. Through it the burden of interpretation is removed from the shoulders of priests and scholars and given to 'Abdu'l-Bahá. Through it the unity of the Faith is at once secured and protected against any conflicting counter interpretations. With the Word thus removed from any single person's control, and simultaneously made available to all, through the parallel exhortations to meditate, to study, to investigate the truth independently, the traditional role of the priest is annulled. He is no longer the keeper of the Word, the interpreter of its mysteries to the illiterate multitudes.

Instead, the power of the priest, curtailed and vastly

controlled, finds itself, in this religion, dispersed among
the various institutions of the Administrative Order.
While single individuals are entirely divested of the
authority of leadership, we find collective bodies instead
– elected by secret ballot and conducting their affairs by
means of consultation – empowered to make decisions
that will affect community life, though will in no way
interfere with individual conscience and worship. Where
individuals rise to a position of eminence, it is made
clear, through the careful instructions of 'Abdu'l-Bahá
and the guidance of Shoghi Effendi, that such people,
however inspiring and learned, however respected and
loved, have no personal authority or power. The
psychology that depends on 'priestcraft' is by these
means gradually weaned away from the need to depend
on others for spiritual decisions and is provided with a
framework that will protect the naive from the manipulation of the unscrupulous.

So much for our ideals. How, one might ask, have we
put them into practice? In order to find out it might be
illuminating to turn to the pages of *The Dawn-Breakers* in
order to watch the struggles of the early Bábís, who in far
more extreme circumstances than we, had to wean
themselves away from 'priestcraft'. For what they were
facing, in the most dramatic and savage way, was the
pain and confusion associated with a break with past
traditions and institutions. And of all traditional institutions the one most keenly felt by them, the one by which
they had been nurtured and now by which they were
being ruthlessly persecuted, was that of the priesthood.
When we see the degree to which they reflected the very
characteristics of this class of people who became their
inveterate enemies, when we see them overwhelmed by

tribulations that seem in retrospect to be designed for the very purpose of shaking them loose from these traditional moorings, when we watch their helplessness as the very structure of search that has led them to discover the truth of the Báb must be undermined for them to vindicate His Name, we may perhaps discover our own dilemmas in theirs and recognize the challenge we face in the many centuries ahead to redefine power and spiritual authority and to assume responsibility for our own fates. Certainly it will take time, and their courage and mistaken zeal provide us with many lessons and raise many questions.

The episode most resonant with unanswered questions about the nature of spiritual leadership and authority, abrogation of traditions and assumption of new roles, occurred at Badasht. It was an episode that, according to the psychological or anthropological sense of the word, can only be described as liminal: an imposed period, or ceremony, or controlled experience during which all preconceived notions are exploded and separated one from the other, all fragments of psyche and society are scattered and reversed, and order re-emerges in a completely different form. According to this definition every divine Revelation is liminal, on a vast cyclic scale. But within each historical period, indeed within each individual life, there are certain liminal episodes of vital significance associated with change in both attitude and expression, being and belief. Most significantly, for the present purposes, liminal experiences in religious and secular terms find their finest expression through drama-tic means, using artifice to create insight.

The conference at Badasht is one such liminal episode in Bahá'í history which may serve in time as a symbol for individual transformation as well as a collective shift of

consciousness. Its importance to the Bábí community, as
we know, was inestimable but its significance was more
far-reaching to history than might have been imagined
by that community. It contains all the elements of a
powerful spiritual conflict couched in an action that is
unashamedly theatrical. The most significant characteristic of this episode is that no matter how many times one
attempts analysis of it, something about the configuration
of events and the confrontation of protagonists, the
words that we hear and the silence that surrounds them,
remains mysterious, unfathomable, defying any final
interpretation. My suggestion that this episode might
illustrate the process of maturation in a community
struggling to free itself from the lime of 'priestcraft' is
certainly not the only way in which these events might be
perceived.

Some of the details which offer the richest source of
ambiguity appear to be the most unimportant. We might
begin for instance by considering the utter insignificance
of the location of this event. Liminal experiences are
frequently associated with places far removed from the
centres of civilization. Islands, such as Prospero's in *The
Tempest*, the dark woods of Dante and Spenser where the
individual loses his old self in order to find his new,
planets spinning in the desolation of space and ships
trapped in silent seas, all share in common a sense of
isolation from society and removal from the plane of
ordinary interaction. Badasht was no exception. A little
village in the middle of a dry Persian plateau; Shoghi
Effendi describes the place as though it were indeed an
island: 'a tiny hamlet in the plain of Badasht on the
border of Mázindarán'.[1] Nabíl records the night-long
journey that it takes, on horseback, before the eighty-one

participants gather 'at the hour of dawn'. The conver-
gence of riders out of the dark, the twelve-hour journey it
takes as they 'set out on horseback that same evening for
that village' in order to arrive 'the next morning at the
hour of sunrise', all serve to isolate the place and
intensify its remoteness from civilization.

Within this little world, however, there are further
distinctions, each – as the ensuing events would suggest –
seemingly isolated from each other. The three gardens
rented by Bahá'u'lláh within the hamlet of Bada<u>sh</u>t are
in some ways as remote from each other as the village is
from any nearby towns. The sense of exclusivity characteristic of each is underscored by Shoghi Effendi's translation of Nabíl:

> Upon His arrival, Bahá'u'lláh rented three gardens,
> one of which He assigned exclusively to the use of
> Quddús, another He set apart for Ṭáhirih and her
> attendant, and reserved the third for Himself.[2]

Furthermore there is in this detail the implication,
emphasized time and again by Shoghi Effendi in his
interpretation of the event, of Bahá'u'lláh's 'directing
force' behind the scenes. The reference in the footnotes of
The Dawn-Breakers to 'Ka<u>sh</u>fu'l-<u>Gh</u>iṭá', which indicates
that Bahá'u'lláh was 'the prime mover and the controlling and directing influence throughout the different
stages of that memorable episode'[3] is confirmed by the
drumming adverbs which Shoghi Effendi chooses as the
bass line of his orchestration of this event. 'It was
Bahá'u'lláh', he writes, 'Who steadily, unerringly, yet
unsuspectedly, steered the course of that memorable
episode and . . . brought [it] to its final and dramatic

climax.' He it was who 'unobtrusively yet effectually presided over that conference'.[4]

One of the central mysteries of this episode, however, is that we cannot tell how many of the events were overtly controlled and how many not. There is something about a liminal experience that alters our preconceptions about freewill and predestination. The extremes seem to meet; the simple facts seem to separate into enigmatic possibilities. In one sense Bahá'u'lláh might be said to have stage-managed the whole event. In another sense His influence is so ubiquitous as to be forever concealed from our analysis. In retrospect, as Nabíl suggests, we might recognize the controlling influence of those extraordinary events, but at the time we could not gauge what we knew, leave alone recognize what others might have guessed.

One element which may be responsible for our uncertainty is that Bahá'u'lláh's presence throughout is mysteriously passive. Although He holds centre stage, at no point does He ever figure as one of the central characters in the drama. On the contrary, His first appearance is as an audience, watching rather than participating as the actions unfold. Prior to this He has been the Author of the new names given to each participant at Badasht, but even in this act Nabíl emphasizes the mystery that surrounds Him, stating that, 'the identity of Him who had bestowed a new name upon each of those who had congregated in that hamlet remained unknown to those who had received them.'[5] The very convolutions of this sentence, its elliptical phrases and side-stepping clauses, seem to imply that such mysteries can only be revealed by indirection, that He Who names us cannot yet be named.

We enter the drama, therefore, enclosed in our narrow limitations, confined to our separate gardens, each of us subject to our own prejudices, each at the mercy of conjectures 'according to his own degree of understanding'. If we perceive the significance of the play we are in, it is dim; if we suspect an Author, it is by mere surmise. Even when we turn to 'the best-informed' account of the occurrences at Badasht, heard at several removes from the one who is said to have reported them, we have little more to consider than the bare outlines of the outer spectacle. The inner significance, like a seed concealed in time, can only bear fruit as we evolve in our own understanding, asking infinite questions, enacting the same process of transformation and change as those who first experienced them at Badasht.

The primary actions that took place at Badasht are too familiar for mere repetition, but there are details associated with those events that cast a curious light on the theme of the present study. What, for example, does this episode tell us about the nature and the dangers of assuming spiritual leadership? How are the traditions of priesthood challenged and why is the participation of a woman so important in this process? What is the import of her words, not only for the future role of her sex, but also for the altered emphasis on 'priestcraft'?

I would like to look closely at what Shoghi Effendi calls the 'dramatic crisis' of Badasht which begins on the day when Bahá'u'lláh is confined to His bed with a mysterious illness. It is hardly profitable to imagine whether or not His illness was premeditated, though there were no doubt some who may have wondered that, at the time and since. What is significant, for me, is that due to this illness all the ensuing action takes place within His garden, compacted within His bed-chamber, contained, as much as possible, beneath His directing gaze. It is His indisposition that causes Quddús to 'hasten to visit Him' where he takes his place 'on the right hand' of Bahá'u'lláh. It is this same cause that draws the remaining companions into the garden, which is neither that allotted to Quddús nor that reserved for Ṭáhirih, and entices them further still into the presence of their Host where they sit or stand 'grouped', as Shoghi Effendi so dramatically translates it, 'around Him'. It is when we see them all there, together, that we are made critically aware of the one highly significant outsider, the woman, Ṭáhirih. It is specifically because she is a woman that she cannot be included in such a gathering. It is her sex that forces her to be apart, with her own companion and attendant, in a separate garden where she may be visited but not joined, from where she might issue messages but not emerge.

At this moment a fascinating interaction takes place which might be forgotten in the excitement that follows and is subsumed in the drama it prologues. A messenger enters, a man who acts as a go-between, an intermediary between the two major protagonists of the drama, although we have no indication from *Nabíl's Narrative* that he is aware of the decision 'previously arrived at between Quddús and Ṭáhirih'[6] about the nature of the message he is asked to carry. He is called Muḥammad-Ḥasan-i-Qazvíní and has, along with the others, recently received a new name; but it seems unlikely, despite his manifest sincerity, that he either understands its significance or the meaning of the message it is his misfortune to carry. Certainly his initial rapid response to commands, followed by his growing anxiety over his difficult role, and his increasing desperation as all efforts to bridge the gap between Ṭáhirih and Quddús prove impotent, testify to his earnest willingness to fulfil an impossible task. He has assumed a new name without having any clear idea of the dilemmas it may pose, and we see him attempting, as it were, to apply the old code of meaning to a set of circumstances that are outside his frame of reference.

His task would seem on first sight to be simple: he has to bring a message from a lady to a gentleman who is in the company of a crowd of men where it would be un-fitting for a lady to be seen. According to the old code, his purpose is twofold: he must ensure the utmost respect be accorded to the lady in this public setting and at the same time he must at all costs maintain respect for the gentleman to whom he is applying for a like courtesy. From the onset, however, none of the old rules seem to apply. The gentleman responds in a fashion that can only be called downright rude, and the lady insists on being appallingly stubborn. Upon delivering his humili-ating message poor Muḥammad-Ḥasan is further afflicted by the unthinkable threat of the lady's imminent arrival: 'If you persist in your refusal,' he tells Quddús, 'she herself will come to you.'[7] It is an alternative that strikes everyone present as entirely inappropriate and which must at all costs be prevented. If either the gentleman or the lady would please remember the proper code all would be well, but some other force seems to be at work, some alternative and entirely superior code seems to be playing havoc with the circumstances.

In addition to the old chivalric code, there is a specifically religious one at work that is rooted in Islamic traditions. The messenger is an intermediary between two spiritual leaders, two priest-like figures in the Bábí community. The fact that one of them is a woman simply adds fuel to the fire. The lady, according to Nabíl, is for many of those present 'the very incarnation of Fátimih, the noblest emblem of chastity in their eyes'[8] and the gentleman is considered 'the sole representative of the Báb'.[9] Also, what very few people other than the gentleman know is that the One in Whose presence they are sitting is Himself of a spiritual stature even more considerable than either Fátimih or the Báb's representative. In addition to the chivalric element of the code, therefore, we find this other dimension, whose Islamic roots point to even greater spiritual codes than can be clearly understood at this juncture.

Muḥammad-Ḥasan has only one recourse, according to the traditional chivalric code he has adopted. When dishonour is offered to an idealized lady by an idealized gentleman, both of whom hold priest-like sway over your soul, you can neither permit yourself to convey that dishonour to her as the messenger nor defy the one who offers it. According to the Islamic code, moreover, in which such dishonour assumes religious dimensions, there is only one solution: self-immolation. Muḥammad-Ḥasan, trapped by the circumstances, falls back on these old codes, unsheathes his sword and lays it at the feet of Quddús. 'Either choose to accompany me to the presence of Ṭáhirih', says the poor man, 'or cut off my head with this sword.'[10]

It is very important that a human life be at stake at this tense moment. We should not forget the vulnerability of that life as we consider the alternatives before us. If we look closely at the motives underlying the behaviour of Quddús and Ṭáhirih in this carefully constructed dilemma, we see illuminated several other factors all of which impinge upon the poor messenger's plight. What is Ṭáhirih doing by insisting that Quddús visit *her*, and by threatening, if he does not, that she must therefore break all rules of decorum and visit *him*? Why is it that Quddús is forcing this issue to become so confrontational? What is there about leaving the present company in order to submit to her requests which makes him use such harsh language in response to Ṭáhirih's message?

Clearly a dramatization of priorities is being enacted here. From Ṭáhirih's point of view it would appear that the whole issue of 'priestcraft' is being questioned, and woman's particular relation to it. She will not sanction the elevation of any one believer over the other. Of Quddús she says, 'I deem him . . . a pupil whom the Báb has sent me to edify and instruct. I regard him in no other light.' In public she rebukes him and confronts him with her daunting equality, refusing to submit to the notion of either his spiritual or sexual superiority. From Quddús' point of view we hear a similar statement about priestcraft. 'I am free to follow the promptings of my own conscience,' he retorts, when reprimanded by Ṭáhirih for his behaviour. 'I am not subject to the will and pleasure of my fellow-disciples.'[11] Both of them, however, provide us with another dimension to the message they are conveying by insisting on staying in or coming to the presence of Bahá'u'lláh. In addition to dramatizing the significance of absolute equality in the sight of God, an equality that totally undermines the need for a priest-hood, they further establish by their actions that there is another kind of leadership, at once mysterious and immediately accessible, that transcends all 'priestcraft' and invalidates all previous priorities.

To leave the presence of Bahá'u'lláh in order to comply with anyone's request, whether man or woman, carries profound implications for the meaning of spiritual leadership. We are leaving the plane of courtesy here and entering at this point the realm of spiritual recognition. No one and nothing can take precedence over one's utter commitment to one's Beloved in this world and the next. Only when viewed in this light, the light of a hyper-sensitive awareness of Bahá'u'lláh's station, can Quddús' apparent callousness be understood to be more than mere male chauvinism. Only when viewed in this light too can Táhirih's insistence on violating feminine codes of behaviour be understood to be more than mere sexual egoism. Certainly many of those present would have been shocked by his rudeness, and many others were equally appalled by her disrespect. Some would have interpreted Quddús' words as an assumption of his own spiritual authority over the community and would have felt, according to the old codes of belief, a complacent satisfaction in what they considered his right to speak this way, particularly to a mere upstart of a woman. Others, keenly aware of Táhirih's station, would have been stunned by this young man's vulgar insensitivity, would have felt a surge of outrage to defend her honour, and so committed the error of falling, for their own part, into the same old codes of reaction. Only by recalling, as an audience, the silent and vital presence throughout all this of the One Observer, Himself unobserved, can we grasp something of the magnitude of change that is impending. Only when we remember the silent Onlooker who watches all and interferes with nothing, whose all-perceiving eye never wavers, never blenches for a moment at the human dilemma being enacted before Him, do we sense, suspended in that lingering moment, the full force of the immense transformation of all human codes, if that change is to occur.

As it is, for that extraordinary moment, all time seems transfixed forever, all action frozen. There lies Muḥammad-Ḥasan at the feet of Quddús, with his neck 'stretched forth . . . to receive the fatal blow'. There is Quddús who has just accepted the sword and is 'willing to comply with the alternative' that has been put before him, namely, that of cutting off the head of the unfortunate man.[12] No one in the present company appears capable of altering the course of these apparently absurd proceedings. No one raises a finger to protect Muḥammad-Ḥasan from the fate he has chosen for himself. No one offers to mediate between Quddús' unyielding attitude and Ṭáhirih's improvident imperatives. And then we realize with awe that Bahá'u'lláh is permitting these proceedings. Why has He allowed this impasse to occur?

There is a powerful symbol implicit in the position of the two men before us – the one holding an unsheathed sword and ready to strike a blow, the other kneeling with his neck prepared to receive it. This particular configuration of human bodies signifies age-old patterns of wretchedness and helplessness. It describes in an almost exaggerated form the exploitations we have enacted throughout history. That archetypal image of the neck outstretched and the sword raised against it illustrates the stale custom of war, the hyperbole of male-dominance, the exaggeration of stubborn prejudices, the posturing and protesting of people on the basis of illusions. It illustrates the result of false choices that have led to our being trapped within the social, religious and political formulas we have created for ourselves over the course of the past several centuries. The inevitability of blind force and violence that it sanctifies, the inflexibility of contradictory ideologies that it illustrates, the confrontation on grounds of imagined religious authority that it dramatizes testify to an impotence universally acknowledged, a paralysis induced by ossified superstition, a rigid code which seems unbreakable. It is this code to which Shoghi Effendi refers in his description of the event we are witnessing as having been 'a sudden, startling, complete emancipation from the dark and embattled forces of fanaticism, of priestcraft, of religious orthodoxy and superstition'.[13] It is also this code that has until the present moment been the established one among men who are 'mostly recruited from the very ranks they were attacking'.[14]

Into this impasse walks Ṭáhirih, 'adorned and unveiled',[15] as the stage directions have it. It is significant that had she walked in a moment later there would have been the blood of more than one man shed that day. For while the consternation and tumult caused by her appearance leads one of those present to cut his throat and run shrieking from the room, Muḥammad-Ḥasan, who was prepared for his death, is spared. Muḥammad-Ḥasan is, in fact, quite forgotten. His bare neck is no longer the focus of anyone's attention, because they are gazing now on a face they have never, in their wildest dreams, imagined they would see. If the messenger is to be remembered at all after this it will be as Fata'l-Qazvíní, for Ṭáhirih's 'sudden and most unexpected apparition'[16] challenges all present to identify themselves by their new names, not their old. All old names, old codes, old dilemmas, together with that most symbolic veil, are swept away. She stands before us beautiful, and unbearably revealed. And together we have been plunged into a new set of dilemmas and have to face in her luminous countenance a new series of questions.

When we look for answers to these questions in the faces of those present we see a bewildering range of responses that to a large measure reflect the ways we have been trying to grapple with the issue of equality and power over the century that has since intervened. We see anger and outrage, we see fear and bewilderment. Amidst all these we see Táhirih's face, luminous, radiant. Her actions too are quiet and dignified. Her 'unruffled serenity' is sharply contrasted 'with the affrighted countenances of those who were gazing upon her face'.[17] The 'feeling of joy and triumph'[18] illuminating her countenance is set against the wordless rage imprinted on the features of Quddús. We see a face splattered with blood and others drained white with stunned shock and we are acutely aware of the Face we do not see. In these faces, and through the presence of the One unseen, it is possible to sense the paradox encompassed by all these extremes.

When the choices are extreme one is either pulled apart by them or finds one can stretch to accommodate them. By conjuring the full range of human reactions within the confines of those circumstances Bahá'u'lláh challenged that community to respond to a new and wider order. By choreographing the episode so that it took place neither in the garden of Quddús nor in that of Táhirih but in His own, He showed that such extremes can only find a meeting ground in the new garden that has appeared. The sexes, separated by custom and superstition for centuries, and priest figures reluctant to

relinquish their powers to each other, can only meet
before One whose spiritual authority far surpasses either
of theirs, Whose very invisibility in the episode enables
us to recognize that He is above the distinctions of sex
and beyond the need for 'priestcraft'.

'Verily,' chants Ṭáhirih, after her eloquent address,
'amid gardens and rivers shall the pious dwell in the seat
of truth, in the presence of the potent King.' Nabíl tells
us that when she uttered these last words 'she cast a
furtive glance towards both Bahá'u'lláh and Quddús in
such a manner that those who were watching her were
unable to tell to which of the two she was alluding.'[19] It
is most significant that this fact too remains a mystery.

Mysteries are not easily resolved at Badasht. The
questions that arise, the contradictions that are voiced,
the tension that ensues is not easily dispelled. It takes
the 'masterly' intervention of Bahá'u'lláh to effect 'a
complete reconciliation' between Ṭáhirih and Quddús,[20]
but even that does not prevent some of the company
who have witnessed this revolution of thought and habit
to indulge in excesses and 'transgress the bounds of
moderation'.[21] Even though the two protagonists of this
drama leave the scene seated in the same howdah 'which
had been prepared for their journey by Bahá'u'lláh',[22]
other individuals both then and since have continued to
play out the clash of extremes symbolized by their
confrontation.

In this group of men, whom some might class as
insignificant religious fanatics gathered in some god-
forsaken village in the middle of the last century, we find
– as the result of the active participation of one woman –
the meeting of archetypes, the clash of elementals, a
confrontation of vast proportions whose psychological

as well as spiritual significance has rocked us for generations since. The question to ask might be, could the same liminal experience have occurred, alerting all those present to the transformation required in attitudes to leadership and spiritual authority, if no woman had been present, or if the protagonists had been of one sex only? What is there about this additional equation of sex that charges the events with a colour and light, a fire and energy that cannot be dimmed? How does the idea of sex tell us something about the shift from an old order into a new? How does it stimulate the cataclysmic change from the customs that have held both men and women in thrall for centuries in ways which no ideology related to economics or even race can do? How does the similarity between a community struggling for its spiritual emancipation and women who are asking for their equal rights force men to grapple with an issue they have been afraid of for centuries? Only by asking the question 'can women be priests?' do both we and they 'shake off the shackles of an antiquated system' that Shoghi Effendi tells us must be discarded in order for us to ask 'why have priests at all?' Only forced by the question of which of them is 'right' do we face the dilemma that we may have been asking the wrong question all along.

4

Fundamentalism

The word 'fundamentalism' has come to be closely associated with religion but has more in common with a certain mental attitude than with religious belief. There is a difference between the spiritual message at the core of a religion and the blind expression of that faith grounded in fear. The word 'fundamentalism', therefore, is a measure of the hold which 'priestcraft' has upon the crowd. It defines our dependency as a collective conscience upon the interpretation of the few elect. It is characterized by our fear of being numbered by them among 'the erring'. While the individual is cautioned in the Bahá'í writings against assuming this kind of authority over others, the group is also being educated and alerted against these habits of fear. But while centuries of religious tradition have already gone into raising as well as refining the consciousness of the individual, we are only at the beginning of the unfolding drama of the evolution of the crowd.

One of the questions we might ask is how, after centuries of tradition, we can be weaned from our dependency on priestcraft. When Marx referred to religion, and by extension to those who wielded authority in its name, as 'the opiate of the people', he was using a metaphor that reflects the addictive qualities which make transformation very hard. Centuries earlier the

Reformation movement had only succeeded in replacing the Pope and his bishops with a substitute, a 'royal priesthood', one in which every sincere believer became a priest, for in Luther's words, 'all we who believe on Christ are kings and priests in Christ'. A congregation of priests, each eager to give a sermon to the congregation, led in turn to the proliferation of Christian sects in the nineteenth century. And a comparative analysis of these many sects reveals that their most distinguishing features are concerned with the power relationships between the individual and the collective conscience. Charismatic leaders, pastors and reverents have vied with each other ever since for control over the faithful. Indeed it may to a large part be due to the resentment of that loss of power that we see a resurgence today of political preachers in both east and west, and a backlash of fundamentalist faiths in which the voice of the priest is once again heard in the land, not quite as gentle as the turtle.

The human psyche, as we have seen, is not only vulnerable to the addiction of wielding power, but to abdicating it. Our century has not only witnessed the creation of individual monsters on the political scene but the proliferation of masses of hypnotized crowds. It may be indeed that totalitarianism in Europe during this century is the grotesque political mask that has replaced an earlier religious one. The face beneath the mask, as Rilke so brilliantly envisaged, is raw and horrifying.[1] It is a face of naked vulnerability, a face that betrays the experience of spiritual rape. It is a face that reflects the terror of choices, the dread of the unknown, and the fear and hatred of itself so intense that it must at all costs find an enemy to hate. We have seen that face looking at us in this century, in Hitler's Germany and Stalin's Russia, in

Mao's China and in the faces of terrorists from the Middle East to the Middle West.

The face of the crowd measures our collective fears and our dependence, our need for leadership and our vulnerability to being different, and, above all, it demands answers for questions which it dreads to ask. Over the past half century we have painfully acquired a degree of political maturity that has given us the courage to ask many questions about the nature of totalitarian regimes and our attraction to them. However, our reluctance to engage in religious debate and our relative ignorance of the profound spiritual reservoirs that are being tapped by religious fundamentalism have left us painfully vulnerable to these acquired habits and wide open to their continued abuse.

The emotional vulnerability, almost spiritual nakedness of the crowd, has been noted time and again as a 'feminine' quality. Like women who need the guidance of a spiritual mentor, like children who are inexperienced and physically helpless, the masses are depicted as having no will of their own, or at least no ability to control that will. Shakespeare's crowds, characterized by those pejoratives usually reserved for women, are frequently described as weak, vacillating, servile, inconstant and stupid. Hitler made the analogy explicit in *Mein Kampf* and as early as 1923 proceeded to act ruthlessly upon the assumption:

Someone who does not understand the intrinsically feminine character of the masses will never be an effective speaker. Ask yourself: 'What does a woman expect from a man?' Clearness, decision, power, and action. What we want is to get the masses to act. Like

a woman, the masses fluctuate between extremes . . .
The crowd is not only like a woman, but women
constitute the most important element in the audience.
The women usually lead, then follow the children, and
at last, when I have already won over the whole family
– follow the fathers.[2]

But the equation can be made to work the other way
too. Perhaps if the role of women in this Faith shook
the foundations of priestcraft, it may be possible for us
to change the nature of our collective dependency also.
The patriarchal foundations of fundamentalism might
well be shaken as the status of women is raised, as their
education, and that of their daughters as well as sons,
is ensured, as they begin to take their active part, not
merely as audience, but as participants in society.

It may be useful at this point to look at the relationships between the role of women and the maturation of
the crowd, the role of theatre and the manipulation of the
audience, and the significance of a spiritual dimension in
the affairs of society. If Hitler was right, and 'the psyche
of the masses' is 'like a woman, whose spiritual sensitive-
ness is determined less by abstract reasoning than by an
indefinable emotional longing for fulfilling power',[3] then
why shouldn't the spiritual sensitivity of the masses
be educated, uplifted? Why can't the crowd feel itself
responsible for its own actions rather than the spectator
of the actions of others? If fundamentalist leaders like
Hitler have been able 'to act as a loudspeaker proclaim-
ing the most secret desires, the least permissible instincts,
the suffering and personal revolts of a whole nation',[4]
then why can't there be ways to resist such acts of mass
rape? What are the other desires and instincts, aspirations

rather than merely revolts which could protect us from being spiritually violated by fundamentalism?

The relationship between the individual and the state, between an actor and a crowd, is what constitutes theatre. I would therefore like to explore these questions primarily through the theatrical metaphor that contains them. The degree to which we recognize our responsibility as a crowd and the degree to which we wean ourselves from dependence on priestcraft, moreover, is the means by which we can measure our development as a Bahá'í community in matters such as equality between the sexes and the recognition of the relativity of truth. By looking briefly at broad theatrical conventions we might be able to grasp something about the process of educating a whole community, about its relationship to the question of equality and the role of fear or anxiety in this process.

Theatre provides a natural means to resolve the questions it raises through the dramatic use of interruption or delay. Theatre does not *answer* questions: it allows them to be heard; it permits for differing, sometimes contradictory interpretations; it invites the clash of opinions and recognizes that difference as dramatically necessary. It is, in brief, a process both emotional and intellectual, which Bahá'ís have been invited to experience within a consultative context – in assembly meetings, at the Nineteen Day Feast, wherever consultation is vital, exciting and real.

Rarely do we accept such daunting invitations. Many times, perhaps due to our lack of trust and fear of the consultative process, we have engaged in rather dull dramas. Our Feasts have been more like restrained church services, our assemblies have produced rather boring sit-coms instead of exciting theatre. Many times, because we are fearful of the fluid process of true consultation during which diverse points of view can reverberate across the wide range of the Bahá'í writings, we do not engage, but remain removed, passive and withdrawn. We have yet to learn that Bahá'í theatre cannot work when individuals dominate, when the majority are passive. We have yet to discover that discussion during a Feast does not have to be tidy or arrive at any conclusions. It is the place to air questions and opinions, not impose strictures and absolute answers. It is a remarkable coincidence that Shoghi Effendi set himself the task of translating Nabíl's *Dawn-Breakers*, that book which he claimed would inspire dramas in the future and whose pages are filled with great actors and hysterical audiences, just at the same time that Hitler was manipulating the crowds in Munich in such a way as to pander to passivity and Brecht was writing his theatrical polemics, seeking to transform audience participation from that passive role.

The common denominator and most vital element in the dramatic equation is the audience. Masses of us are still carrying the illusion that we have the passive role and are mere watchers of the spectacle. We want someone else to carry the blame and feel the guilt and bear the responsibility for how we act when confronted by fears. Since we cling to a passive role, it is easy to see how traditional drama can offer us relief. Safe in the audience we can watch others play out our dread. Concealed in the anonymity of the crowd we observe the terrible isolation of individuals facing the unknown.

Much has been written in recent literary criticism

about the links between the use made of anxiety in
theatrical tradition and public executions. The public
execution was an expression of defiance against the state
and also a means of keeping rebelliousness in check. The
condemned prisoner symbolized the subversive element
of society, and as such, assumed the 'feminine' role,
sometimes provoked by the terror of death to repentance,
often brutalized to remain obdurate to the last. The
executioner would represent the power of the state, and
his raised sword, the method by which he brought it
down on the victim's neck, the manner in which he
responded to the prisoner were all vicarious expressions
of the justice of the state. The crowd might experience
terror with the prisoner as well as pity for him, but when
it was drawn to identify with that absolute power, it took
over where the executioner left off and gave vent to its
own frustrations.

The public execution, moreover, contained all the
basic ingredients of folk drama. The plot of the drama
was always known beforehand, the characters were the
bare minimum and their words usually inevitable. Even
when there was no actual stage on which such executions
took place, people would climb up to whatever point of
prominence they could find and create an amphitheatre
looking down from the rooftops. What made the drama
all the more memorable, and provoked the maximum
response from the crowd, was when the clichés of the plot
were slightly altered, the characters different from the
norm, and their words surprising, disturbing, unexpected.

The public theatre was an arena in which the anxiety
of control could be played out between the state and the
watching crowd. It is interesting that the violence of the
crowd at public executions occurs less in countries where

there is a state-sanctioned public theatre, however brutal those public executions might be, such as in England in the sixteenth and seventeenth centuries, where drama had found economic and artistic legitimacy. This was not the case in Iran in the last century or in any Islamic country, where there is no public theatre. The passion plays enacted in secret during the month of Muḥarram were intended to be performed rather than watched; spectators of such sacred activities might have been killed by the zeal of those assuming the roles of the holy martyrs for, according to the Qur'án, to make images of God was a blasphemy, and the act of detached observation implied such a blasphemy. This may be why, during public executions, the crowd felt compelled to cross the line from spectatorship and become participants in the drama, and indeed why the closer the spectacle of execution came to reflecting those holy and sacred rites, the more easily their passions might have been stirred.

Most public executions contained the same elements of violence, blood and remorse as would have been found in these passion plays. It might be guessed that in the executions of some of the Bábís, who were so eloquent as they died and who had committed no felony beside their faith, this similarity was dangerous. The deaths of those being punished for their sacrilege against Islám, and the deaths of the exponents of that holiness depicted in the passion plays, were so alike that the mob would be easily aroused to a pitch of bewilderment, fear, fury and frustration that could only have been released by the most extreme enactment of savagery.

At times like this salutary anxiety finds itself subverted. The awful question left hanging in the air – 'Did they die innocent?' – provokes a fear much more dramatic, and its implication of having made some terrible mistake becomes unbearable.

The questions implicit in this subversive form of theatre concern interpretation. Have we misunderstood something important? Have we erred in judgement? Are we wrong? When a man is killed with a prayer of forgiveness on his lips for the crimes of those who are killing him, we must question social justice. When another is killed for sacrilegious heresy and dies in a spirit of devout humility, his whole being illumined with faith, we must question orthodox religion. When a person condemned as a stirrer-up of mischief, a provoker of sedition, an instigator of social chaos dies quoting poetry, we begin to wonder about all our values. When the brutality, the gore and the violence directed at these people serve merely to make them laugh and clap their hands and dance towards death, we must either question their sanity or our own. Underlying all these reversals is the basic terror of having been gulled, duped, made fools of, raped of our right judgement.

It takes a long time for a crowd to learn the meaning of such reversals. The crowd watching the death in 1850 of the seven Bábís who came to be called the Seven Martyrs of Ṭihrán was no exception. This event is not only significant for Bahá'ís but retains a place in the history of public executions because it has the rather notorious privilege of being the first occasion that an execution was public in Persia. Before this the condemned were brought before the Sháh and put to death gruesomely and privately, for the enjoyment of his eyes alone. With the persecutions of the Bábís, and under the pressure of both the Russian and British Ministers who sought by

this means to enlighten the Sháh from barbaric practices,
the seven men who were martyred before the crowds in
Ṭihrán were literally asked to perform a public drama of
a scope and magnitude never witnessed before.[5] Their
scene of martyrdom might even come to be recognized as
the genesis of a new dramatic tradition in Persian culture
which had never had the opportunity to flourish before. I
would like to look at this episode closely in order to
explore the question of interpretation which the crowd
faces, and its fear of being wrong.

There are some dazzling individuals in the pages of *The
Dawn-Breakers* and there are some notorious crowds. One
can learn a great deal from both. One of the many acts in
the drama between them begins in February of the year
1850 when a list of names of the Bábís is submitted
to Maḥmúd Khán-i-Kalantar in Ṭihrán and fourteen
people are seized and brought to the authorities. Nabíl
himself was in the city at that time and received a
message from Bahá'u'lláh that charged him to remove
himself immediately from danger and return to his
family in Zarand. His father was moreover in a terrible
state of anxiety as he had heard rumours that Nabíl had
already been executed. Therefore in order to comply
with Bahá'u'lláh's directives as well as to allay the trepi-
dation of his family, Nabíl leaves the city and celebrates
the feast of Naw-Rúz in the provinces.

Although the anxiety of his father is relieved, his
own intensifies, heightened in contrast to the festivities
around him. In spite of the solicitude of his parents, he is
oppressed with worry thinking about the plight of 'that
little band' of Bábís in Ṭihrán.

The terrible suspense under which I lived . . . was

unexpectedly relieved by the arrival of Ṣádiq-i-Tabrízí, who came from Ṭihrán and was received in the house of my father. Though delivering me from the uncertainties which had been weighing so heavily upon me, he, to my profound horror, unfolded to my ears a tale of such terrifying cruelty that the anxieties of suspense paled before the ghastly light which that lurid story cast upon my heart.[6]

We are thus prepared, in what follows, to discover an evolution in anxiety, a building up of suspense. Nabíl tells us that under pressure of execution seven of the fourteen prisoners were compelled to recant their faith. The remaining seven are described one by one, with an increasing intensification that is not only reflected in the number of pages allotted to each, but also the content ascribed to every reference. We spend three and four pages on the first two martyrs, a little over one page on the second two and find ourselves stumbling through three brief paragraphs on the last three, who vie with one another to die first. The effect of this is to shift our sense of time. With the first two martyrs we are not only given an account of their lives and the manner in which they heard and accepted their deaths but also the procedure of their trials. As we turn to the others, however, the travesty of justice is graphically depicted by simple omission. The Amír-Nizám who is responsible for judging each case responds to the challenge with characteristic impatience:

No need to bring any more members of this hateful sect before me. Words are powerless to overcome their unswerving obstinacy.[7]

As each man's life is being summed up, less and less

time is allotted to his words and actions, the history of his commitment to his faith. Moment by moment our view of human existence and what seems most important in it is contracted. Increasingly the pressure of immediacy is made to bear upon us; increasingly we are reminded of their impending death; increasingly we concentrate on how they meet their end. The last breath is all.

At the scaffold we are granted their own words, like a testament. They are given a chance to vindicate themselves and bear witness to their commitment to the Cause, and when that chance is cut short by the executioner, once in mid-prayer and another time in mid-proof, it feels almost as though the man's will and testament is being violated.

There is, in addition, a direct relationship between them and the executioner, who becomes the abstract of death itself. In the case of the first martyr, Khál-i-A'zam, whose last words are a prayer for the forgiveness of the executioner's sins, the relationship is particularly dramatic. The executioner is stirred to his very depths and 'pretending that the sword he had been holding in readiness in his hands required to be resharpened, he hastily went away, determined never to return again'.[8]

He cannot make his escape so readily, however, and is forced to commit the crime for which his victim has prayed he be forgiven. Haunted by the deed, he leaves for Khurásán shortly thereafter and takes up the profession of a porter and crier, preferring to carry people's burdens than be burdened with the taking of their lives:

'When I was appointed to this [the executioner's] service,' he was heard to complain, weeping bitterly the while, 'they undertook to deliver into my hands only those who had been convicted of murder and highway robbery. I am now ordered by them to shed the blood of one no less holy than the Imám Músáy-i-Kázim himself!'[9]

Besides serving to transpose us from the narrative to the dramatic mode and heightening our awareness of being an audience with the crowd that watches, the intensification of description has the curious effect of conflating these seven lives into one life. By returning to the fact of death seven times and with increasing and finally dizzying speed, we are given a fleeting glimpse of our own lives and our own most imminent deaths. The tendency, too, that these men have of addressing the dead lying at their feet, of envying their condition, of embracing the prisoner who has been killed before them, all serve to give us an uncanny sensation that 'in their death they were not divided'. When Mírzá Qurbán-'Alí sees the body of his fellow martyr he greets it with feverish joy and holds it in his arms. 'Approach,' he cries out to the executioner, 'and strike your blow, for my faithful comrade is unwilling to release himself from my embrace, and calls me to hasten together with him to the court of the Well-Beloved!'[10] The third martyr who follows these two lying entwined in one another's arms calls out to them with similar greeting. 'Well done, beloved companions!' he cries. 'You have turned Tihrán into a paradise! Would that I had preceded you!'[11] With the last three martyrs we have the extraordinary scene of three men vying to die first, each demanding that the executioner let him hurry after his brothers, each pleading for release before the others.

Their eagerness to precede one another in laying down their lives for their Faith astonished the multitude who wondered which of the three would be preferred to his companions. They pleaded with such fervour that eventually they were beheaded, all three, at one and the same moment.[12]

After such a finale the sense of anti-climax is almost palpable. To raise the expectations to such a pitch only to escape and leave the murmurous crowd with nothing but its own turbulent emotions is a masterstroke in theatre. Only this is real life. Or rather death. Suddenly we are the ones who feel left behind, as if we made some mistake. As a crowd we feel profoundly disturbed, dislocated, somehow alienated. Have we been cheated? Are we being made fools of? We glance round at each other, uneasily, hearts pounding, dreading the feeling that we have been wrong all along. Something unexpected has happened here. This has been no ordinary execution we have been watching. It felt, in fact, as though we were the ones being watched. We were being judged for something done that we did not entirely comprehend. There seemed to be a vast concourse pressed around us, watching our puny drama with pity and disgust, an innumerable throng of witnesses into whose shimmering ranks these martyrs have been welcomed. It makes an audience very anxious to find it is being observed. There are crowds beyond the crowds we are.

At this point I feel compelled, as Nabíl was, to break off from this episode and recall another. The reason I am doing it is because I was forcefully reminded, through the repetition of the gestures – one man kneeling for execution, another man with a sword raised above him and the crowd watching – of the conference of Badasht.

Here, seven times repeated, is the archetypal interaction that was unbearable seen even once, between Quddús and the messenger from Ṭáhirih. Here in most bloody evidence is what happens when Ṭáhirih does not interrupt the proceedings.

But, curiously, Bahá'u'lláh does. It is a detail of considerable wonder to me, even as I was reminded of that historic drama which had taken place two years earlier, to find that Nabíl breaks off his narrative – with the seven bodies lying headless in their gore and the crowd about to lose its own head in its madness – in order to step back from the drama and record it. He had used the word 'suspense' himself to describe his own condition in Zarand with his family. Now surely he has left the crowd in even greater suspense. The reader too is taken unawares by this interruption, all the more so because Nabíl breaks off in order to leap ahead and bring us to the chronicled present.

It is December 1888, one hundred years ago in the past and twenty years into the future from the moment we have just been witnessing. Nabíl is in his home in the prison-city of 'Akká and speaks with an immediacy which Shoghi Effendi preserves some forty years later as he translates and reorganizes this extraordinary work:

'At this stage of my narrative', he writes, 'I was privileged to submit to Bahá'u'lláh such sections of my work as I had already revised and completed. How abundantly have my labours been rewarded by Him whose favour alone I seek, and for whose satisfaction I have addressed myself to this task! He graciously summoned me to His presence and vouchsafed me his blessings'.[13]

What then follows is 'the gist of His words to me on

that memorable occasion'. We find Bahá'u'lláh speaking. The story of the Seven Martyrs hovers unresolved
while we lean forward to hear what He has to say,
forgetful of all else. What He has to say refers to the
circumstances attending the gatherings at Bada<u>sh</u>t. He
introduces Ṭáhirih into the scene.

They anticipate one's every thought, these mysterious
Beings.

It is more than curious.

Was Someone watching us read, we wonder?

We find ourselves reliving the well-known episode, this
time from Bahá'u'lláh's point of view, and with the
hindsight of forty years. But more curious than anything
else is that in His version the sequence which had so
struck our previous narrator, <u>Sh</u>ay<u>kh</u> Abú-Turáb – the
episode of conflict between Quddús and Ṭáhirih, the
episode involving the messenger, and that dramatic
moment of entry when our attention was riveted to the
sword about to fall on his neck – that section is entirely
left out.

But is it? We already knew, according to <u>Sh</u>oghi
Effendi's interpretation, that that whole piece of stage
business was an illusion intended to dramatize the
conflict between the old and the new religions. The life of
Muḥammad-Ḥasan-i-Qazvíní had never been at stake; it
was the fate of this new religion that was in question. The
most important issue was the comprehension of the
Bábís of the immense courage that was needed if they
were to establish the independent nature of their Faith.
On the other hand, we have just been watching that very
episode re-enacted in Ṭihrán, seven times over. Even
though Bahá'u'lláh says nothing about it, the blow that
has fallen repeatedly on the necks of those seven martyrs

in the pages that have just been read imposes itself, like an indelible transparency, on the familiar scene. We could never forget it.

Bahá'u'lláh, however, is not concerned with repetition but progression. He has read all of Nabíl's work up until this point, as we have. He has provided Nabíl with a critique and encouragement. Now He is urging him to record for posterity what He feels was significant about the conference of Badasht. By re-focusing our attention on this episode and re-adjusting our vision so that we see it clearly, from His perspective, He draws our attention to what Shaykh Abú-Turáb has missed. He directs our attention away from the dramatization of polarities and emphasizes instead three issues. The first is the prophetic significance of Ṭáhirih's gesture and His assumption of the role of guardian and protector over her. The second is the unspeakable fury, bewilderment and turmoil this action unleashed both within the Bábí ranks and without. And the third is the question of interpretation. These three issues, we discover in retrospect, are absolutely vital to our understanding of the story of the Seven Martyrs of Ṭihrán. They are also vital clues to the question of mistaken interpretation and the education of the crowd which is watching in that story.

The prophetic nature of Ṭáhirih's gesture Bahá'u'lláh illustrates by His reference to the Islamic tradition concerning Fáṭimih, Muḥammad's daughter, who will appear unveiled as she crosses the bridge Sirát on the Day of Judgement. Ṭáhirih has fulfilled that prophecy and Bahá'u'lláh validates the fulfilment. He champions Ṭáhirih's cause, protects her reputation and, by under-scoring the divinely-ordained nature of her action, supports the claims she has made. In so doing, He

mysteriously re-introduces her *absence* into the episode we
have just witnessed. We become keenly aware that the
terrible waste of human life, the misinterpretations of
spiritual faith, and the vulnerability of the crowd to the
instigation of rabble-rousing priests is in some mysterious way connected to Ṭáhirih's absence.

He begins by recalling that forty years earlier, while
He was engaged in celebrating the nuptials of a certain
prince, the father of the Báb's amanuensis arrived at the
door, interrupting the proceedings in his anxiety to speak
to Bahá'u'lláh. Thus, even in Bahá'u'lláh's story, itself
an interruption of Nabíl's tale of the Seven Martyrs, we
have from the onset the principle established of interruption and delay, both vital to dramatic action. In both
cases, too, such an interruption compels patience, which
is an essential element in respect to that much larger
question here about the means for the maturation of the
crowd. It takes time. The messenger is motioned to wait
and only when the meeting has dispersed can he deliver
his message which concerns Ṭáhirih's imprisonment and
the threat to her life.

At this point we should be conscious that the different
temporal levels of narrative are curiously overlaid, one
on top of the other, like a kind of rich layering of
embroidered lace. When Nabíl began telling us about the
Seven Martyrs of Ṭihrán we knew that Ṭáhirih was
among those imprisoned in the house of Maḥmúd Khán-
i-Kalantar between 14 February and 15 March of the
year 1850, confined, according to our chronicler, on the
upper floor of that same house. All through the ensuing
tale of trial, condemnation and death, therefore, her
presence has been felt, and our anxiety about her fate has
been growing. When Bahá'u'lláh's interruption takes the

narrative back two years earlier we are fully prepared for
the message that her life is in danger. Even as we read of
Bahá'u'lláh's rescue, His plan for her accommodation
and journey to Khurásán, His arrangement for her
attendance at the conference of Badasht, it is easy to
conflate time and wish that He were at hand once more,
in 1850, to come to her rescue.

When we read His brief synopsis of the cataclysmic
events at Badasht on that day when He was confined to
His bed, we are struck by a single most significant fact:
according to Him, the motives underlying Ṭáhirih's
request are entirely different from what we had earlier
imagined. There is no reference to the messenger, nor
even any mention of Quddús. Bahá'u'lláh Himself was
the object of her request. His response is most interesting:
'We were surprised at her message,' He says, 'and were
at a loss as to what We should reply.'[14]

Could it be that Ṭáhirih has written the script for this
part of the drama herself? Clearly she was inspired, for
when she appears suddenly at the door, Bahá'u'lláh
directs our gaze not at her, nor even to the reactions
around her, but rather to the prophecy she has fulfilled.
He chooses to quote His own amanuensis, Mírzá Áqá
Ján, at this point:

> 'The face of Fáṭimih,' he said, 'must needs be revealed
> on the Day of Judgement and appear unveiled before
> the eyes of men. At that moment the voice of the
> Unseen shall be heard saying: "Turn your eyes away
> from that which ye have seen."'[15]

Once he has established beyond all doubt that
Ṭáhirih's gesture belonged not only to this material stage
but coincided with the script of a divine drama already

written, and once we, ourselves both audience and actors
of that larger drama, realize that the suspense and the
delay, the play on expectation and on time, are all part
of the dramatic and salutary experience which makes
this true art, He proceeds to the second issue. We find
Him concentrating not on the rightness or wrongness
of Ṭáhirih's act, but on people's interpretation of prophecy fulfilled. It is the violent reaction of the Bábís that
He stresses, the even more violent response of the mullá
and people at the town of Ámul, and the fact that 'our
friends eventually dispersed, leaving Us at the mercy
of Our enemies'.[16] Shaykh Abú-Turáb's account was,
in His estimation, not strong enough nor was his courage adequate in facing the consequences of this heroic
moment. He attempts to dissuade Bahá'u'lláh from
continuing to keep Ṭáhirih under the shelter of His
protection and delivering her from this uproar by
conducting her back to Ṭihrán. 'That Shaykh', He
concludes,

> was a kind-hearted man, was simple and lowly in
> temper, and behaved with great dignity. He lacked
> courage and determination however, and betrayed
> weakness on certain occasions.[17]

Clearly the Shaykh's account, taken up with the action
on the stage, missed the larger significance behind it.
Identifying through his own weaknesses perhaps with
the plight of the messenger, mesmerized by the unveiled
face of Ṭáhirih on the one hand and the naked sword of
Quddús on the other, he misses the point. Bahá'u'lláh
draws our attention to the immense spiritual power that
Ṭáhirih has unleashed, instead of to her face: 'Turn your
eyes away from that which ye have seen.' In His version

of Bada<u>sh</u>t the arrival of the woman in this archetypal drama highlights that additional dimension of spiritual awareness without which actions can only have a limited interpretation.

We must remember that <u>Shaykh</u> Abú-Turáb was a member of the audience at Bada<u>sh</u>t. He was one among the crowd who began as spectators and ended as actors in that drama, and it is therefore with the response of the crowd that Bahá'u'lláh seems concerned. The final detail He adds to the account which is missing from the <u>Shaykh</u>'s version occurs in Ámul, in the wake of the turmoil at Bada<u>sh</u>t, and is very important for what it tells us about the dilemma of interpretation facing a crowd. He has stressed the unpremeditated source of Ṭáhirih's act. He has confirmed its divinely-inspired nature and, through His consequent protection and custody of Ṭáhirih, given her His whole-hearted approval. Then He tells of the panic of the Bábís who removed themselves to a deserted castle, and shows the reactions of the crowd of over four thousand people at Ámul, who, aroused by the bitter denunciations of the mullá, turn on Him with rage and stones when He attempts to leave that town. This mullá accuses Bahá'u'lláh and His companions of perverting the Faith of Islám and supports his attack by recounting a dream.

Last night I saw you in a dream enter the masjid, which was thronged by an eager multitude that had gathered to witness your arrival. As the crowd pressed round you, I beheld, and lo, the Qá'im was standing in a corner with His gaze fixed upon your countenance, His features betraying great surprise. This dream I regard as evidence of your having deviated from the path of Truth.[18]

Bahá'u'lláh suggests to him an alternative interpretation. In fact, everything about Bahá'u'lláh's interpolation
set by Shoghi Effendi within the context of the story of
the Seven Martyrs of Ṭihrán seems to suggest the vital
principle of the relativity of truth and the significance of
alternative ways of looking at the same events. His
version of the story forces us to consider many contrasts
with Shaykh Abú-Turáb's version. His pattern of
repeated interruption and re-evaluation of past events
demands those habits of thought in the reader/spectator.
Now His interpretation of the mullá's dream requires
a similar relinquishment from a single, dogmatic point
of view. How if that expression of surprise in the mullá's
dream were a sign of the Qá'im's dismay at the treat-
ment that was being meted out to the Bábís? How if the
displeasure were in fact being directed at the mullá himself, since it was after all his dream? The mullá doesn't
like that version at all. He 'rejected Our testimony',
recalls Bahá'u'lláh, 'as a perversion of the truth'.[19] This
leads to confinement and a narrow escape, but the crowd
hear of it and, choosing the mullá's interpretation,
assault Bahá'u'lláh as He tries to leave the town:

> No sooner were the inhabitants informed of this act
> than they arose against Us, besieged the governor's
> residence, pelted Us with stones, and hurled in Our
> face the foulest invectives.[20]

At this point there can be no further divine intervention to give the crowd benefit of the doubt, to provide
another delay, another hopeful interruption to the
tragedy. The violence of the crowd at Ámul recalls that
other crowd who have been watching the executions of
the Seven Martyrs of Ṭihrán, and are now seething with

pent up rage and bewilderment. In fact by this time so
many crowds have been jostling in our minds they have
all converged and it is difficult to distinguish among
them. The crowd in Ámul with their stones have
prepared us for the violence of the crowd in Ṭihrán. But
there was also a dream crowd standing eager to witness
the arrival of Bahá'u'lláh, according to the mullá's
account, and that other invisible host we sense around us
who witness the ensuing events with the same dismayed
surprise which the mullá found recorded on the features
of the Qá'im in his dream.

The question of the crowd's responsibility in interpret-
ing events constitutes one of the purposes of Bahá'u'lláh's
interpolation. It seems that the crowd invariably misses
the spiritual dimension in an event. In telling the story
of the Seven Martyrs, as we noted, Ṭáhirih is introduced
by a kind of *deus ex machina* intervention; in the scene itself
she is tragically absent both symbolically and spiritually.
Like Shaykh Abú-Turáb himself, whose account of
Badasht pales to insignificance beside Bahá'u'lláh's own,
the crowd betrays its vacillating nature in the shift from
well-meaning concern to cowardly rejection. Ironically,
it is only if the symbolic Ṭáhirih, the unveiled embodiment of spiritual awareness, could be recalled that
the crowd might transcend its traditional 'womanish'
response. As it is we recognize Hitler's rallies in the
easily-aroused emotionalism of the crowd in Ṭihrán.

Although initially expressing feelings of indignation
and sympathy on occasion, and giving vent to 'cries of
sorrow and lamentation' reflecting a distress 'that was
reminiscent of the outbursts of grief with which every
year the populace greets the day of 'Ashúrá',[21] nevertheless, the dimension of spiritual awareness is entirely

superficial and the mood of the crowd who witnessed the martyrdom of those seven in Ṭihrán quickly shifts to ugly anger. When the victims, expressing emotions of unutterable joy and eagerness, embrace their execution and appear to escape the clutch of the law by so doing, the crowd goes wild. According to 'Abdu'l-Bahá in *A Traveller's Narrative*, 'the rabble onlookers, awed for a while by the patient courage of the martyrs, again allowed their ferocious fanaticism to break out in insults to the mortal remains of those whose spirits had now passed beyond the power of their malice.'[22] Then, as Nabíl records, in his return to the story which the episode about Badasht had interrupted, for three days and nights,

> Thousands of devout shí'ahs gathered round their corpses, kicked them with their feet, and spat upon their faces. They were pelted, cursed, and mocked by the angry multitude. Heaps of refuse were flung upon their remains by the bystanders, and the foulest atrocities were perpetrated upon their bodies. No voice was raised in protest, no hand was stretched to stay the arm of the barbarous oppressor.[23]

In this grotesque ritual we see the transformation of people into the brute mob, the hydra-headed multitude. We see the ugly face of fundamentalism incited by the fear of being wrong. And we cannot turn away and say we'll have nothing to do with it, because face to face with this unspeakable brutality we have to recognize in ourselves another crowd of onlookers. Nor are we alone. Like the crowd in the mullá's dream, like the crowd too at Badasht, we are in the presence of the Qá'im. Nabíl's chronicle shifts to the Báb's perspective at this point and

we look back through His eyes at the spectacle of carnage
we have just witnessed. No sooner have the bodies of
these seven 'united in body, as they had been in spirit
during the days of their earthly life'[24] been laid to rest in
the same grave than we become conscious of the effects of
this spectacle on the Báb. When He hears of it, Nabíl
tells us, it was 'an added blow'[25] to His already deeply
saddened heart which has been sorrowing over the
sufferings of the believers at Ṭabarsí. We can hardly bear
to see the expression on His face, the dismay and grief
reflected there. How we choose to interpret these signs
becomes vitally important, as important as it was to the
mullá of Ámul, for the drama of our own involvement
now begins. We can no longer be spectators.

5

Fear

'We will give over the house,' cry the two daughters whose father left them and their brother with debts as an inheritance.[1] 'We will give over the house and all its contents to Mírzá Músá.' Mírzá Músá was their brother and, unlike his sisters, was a Bahá'í, but had been made to believe through the gossip of the Persian community in Baghdád, and in particular the insinuations of 'the latter-day mujtahids', that his two sisters had absconded with his father's ready cash. It was by inducing such quarrels among the heirs that these unscrupulous people hoped themselves to accumulate the spoils. Now, rising to the bait, the two outraged sisters gather the remnants of their dignity about them and lash back at their brother. 'We will give over the house and all its contents to Mírzá Músá,' they cry, stung with rancour. 'We two will leave the house, with nothing but our veils.'

The two girls are not quite as forlorn nor as self-denying as they might appear at this point. They have just made incredible nuisances of themselves at the home of Bahá'u'lláh, arriving with another relative who 'settled down in the public reception rooms' for a week, taking over the family apartments with their importunate cries for help, clamouring morning and night for Bahá'u'lláh's intervention in their affairs in order that justice might be done with regard to their father's estate.

Because of their refined tastes and expectations –
'Abdu'l-Bahá tells us in *Memorials of the Faithful* that they
have been 'accustomed to the best of everything [and]
could hardly be satisfied with bread and water' – the
family of Bahá'u'lláh, who live with the bare essentials,
are pressed into debt through this solicited hospitality.
'Food had to be procured for them on credit,' admits
'Abdu'l-Bahá. 'Briefly, from every direction, there were
problems.'

At the point in the story where we have just met them,
confronting these accusations levelled at their honesty
and protesting upon their outraged honour that they will
hand everything over and 'leave the house with nothing
but our veils', these two ladies and their brother are
standing in the middle of the family house, surrounded
by jewellers and accountants and a whole crowd of
hangers-on and other experts who are busy making
appraisals, collecting together *objets d'art* and costly
furnishings, analyzing ledger books and eavesdropping.
The effects of the deceased have been carefully divided,
according to 'Abdu'l-Bahá's instructions, and He has
just discovered that because He did not personally
supervise this process, three lots have been drawn up
instead of two. 'One share is for Mírzá Músá,' they tell
him, 'one for the two daughters, and the third', – and
here no doubt the eavesdroppers all prick up their ears –
'the third we place at Your disposal.' When He protests
that His instructions should have been obeyed and the
inheritance divided simply into two equal halves, one for
the son and the other for the two daughters to share
which would have been the expected custom, they insist
on their desire to include Him on the grounds that their
father had 'conceived a remarkable love for Bahá'u'lláh'

and since 'this third is the portion of the deceased . . . You are to expend it in any way You see fit.'

After much volubility and *ta'áruf* with 'Abdu'l-Bahá adamant that He will in no way accept 'so much as a copper coin' and the brother and sisters protesting with hyperbolic insistence that indeed He must, the issue of ready cash is raised. The brother wants to know where his father's ready cash has been kept. The two sisters claim they know nothing about any ready cash. Minutes after they have been pressing the dubious third of their inheritance on the Master with unctuous tones and extravagant flattery, they fall into accusation and counter-protestation on the grounds of this ugly disagreement and make a public scene of their quarrel. The jewellers and other appraisers must have been wonderfully enter-tained. Finally the sisters, smarting with the offensive suggestion that they have done away with the money, incensed with righteous indignation, galled by the acutely embarrassing position they have been forced into, take umbrage in these ultimate terms. A century later we can still hear their bitterness, their tone of in-jured pride: 'We two will leave the house, with nothing but our veils.'

'Abdu'l-Bahá could see that further debate on this matter 'would lead to a scandal and produce nothing of value'. Bahá'u'lláh had known it would lead to such an impasse and had earlier declared 'with finality that intervention in affairs of this kind was abhorrent to Him'. But after consultation with Him a solution was found so that by the end of the day there was 'no residue of complaints, no uproar, no further quarrels'. As 'Abdu'l-Bahá reports to His father, on His return, 'it was accomplished only through Your confirmations. Otherwise it could not have been completed in a year.' The much-debated third portion goes to pay all the son's debts 'so that', Bahá'u'lláh is reported to have said, Mírzá Músá 'may be at peace with his sisters.' The veil is carefully drawn across his suspicions. His own portion, as many expected, was soon scattered to the winds and within a short while the Government confiscated all his properties and sold them for next to nothing. All that remains of the inheritance is the last portion, that belonging to the sisters, who pocket their jewels, adjust their veils and disappear from the story.

The significance of the veil for women is richly illustrated in this story. Certainly it is a liability. Those with veils have to share their inheritance; those without can squander twice as much as they deserve. But the veil is also useful. When the ladies withdraw into its anonymity they can no longer be hounded, no longer accused. No questions of morality can probe those all-concealing folds. No one would venture to lift the veil to advertise the cupidity beneath it without demonstrating his own. It is their curse, but it is also their last refuge. And when they cry out against the cruel world that has misjudged their integrity, when they renounce all claim to costly furnishings, when they give up, at least rhetorically, their share of the inheritance, limited as it is, they do not give up their veils. Their veils are symbols of their honourable virtue, their dignified poverty, their family pride. Above all they are symbols of all that they wish to shield themselves from, all that they fear. They claim to renounce the world but hang on to their self-interests. 'We two will leave the house, with nothing but our veils.'

'Nothing but our veils' is a great deal too much in the

circumstances. It is precisely such forms of false security, such postures of pretence against fear that we have to give up. But in order to be free of such veils we need first to recognize the nature of our fears. Fear has forged chains both literal and psychological and is of three major kinds. There is the generalized fear of the unknown that leads to existential questions about who we are and what our lives are for. There is the fear of responsibility which governs the roots of blame and guilt in our lives and leads to violence in society. And there is fear of the 'other', at which this violence is directed and in opposition to which it is harnessed.

It is one of our characteristics, as a species, to turn to platitudes when considering uncomfortable subjects. Perhaps it is even a genetically programmed response we have in order to ensure the survival of the human race for whom total recall without the benefit of cliché might be more catastrophic than any nuclear explosion. In any event, it is customary for us to refer to death as the 'significant unknown' of our lives. It is easier for us to consider death as a euphemism, as a mysteriously elevated inevitability, rather than as the stark jolt of recollected transience that it is. In spite of our careful euphemisms, however, considering death is not something we would choose to do on a daily basis. It generally sneaks up on us unawares, and suddenly, there we are, considering death. But we don't normally plan on it.

Nevertheless, both religion and philosophy, and most recently psychology, economics and the politics of nuclear deterrence, all ask us to consider it. Indeed, given the rising number of teenage suicides, perhaps we ought to consider introducing death studies into the educational curriculum, replacing one hour of physical education each week with a meditation on our physical demise. Certainly all the counselling and programming and special services and legal aid and whatever other useful social and psychological veils we construct cannot help us avoid it.

In our times, however, the fear of death or the unknown has been amplified from previous mere existential proportions to massive global dimensions. Since the nuclear threat is so impossible to contain it frequently leads us to lose all sense of responsibility for our lives. Consequently, we are terrorized by anxiety, by the fear of assuming personal responsibility. For who can claim to comprehend the consequences of – leave alone assume responsibility for – the environmental crises, the population explosions, the drug and alcohol abuse in vast urban proportions, and the widening gap between the poor and wealthy peoples of the earth? No wonder teenagers commit suicide. The complexity of all these issues seems to transcend anyone's personal efforts to assist in their solution, and so the 'normal' reaction is to abdicate. The two sisters' reaction to trouble was in a sense prophetic. They were basically saying, 'We don't want to have any more to do with the mess.'

But nothing is as easy as it might at first seem. Whenever we are afflicted by deep-rooted fears, our systems of thought tend towards over-simplistic rigidity. We put up the barricades; we haul out the artillery. Fundamentalism, as we have already seen, becomes a means of protecting ourselves from the flux of contradictory ideas, the whirl of paradoxes. Our sense of powerlessness, our need for assurance, our dread of extinction all find short-term relief in the absolutist mentality of right and wrong, heaven and hell. And in this Manichean universe it is always useful to have a scapegoat.

Finding scapegoats, as any tyrant knows instinctively, is an essential way to bend the energies of a nation to egocentric and warped ends. Religious as well as political leaders have frequently tried to take advantage of our collective instinct to abdicate, as well as our anxiety caused by thoughts of death and cosmic impotence, by bending these to their own ends. The *momento mori* tradition, the practice of the detailed visualization of Christ's death on the cross in the Catholic faith, the doctrine of self-mortification associated with various religions both of the East and the West, are all attempts, by the established priesthood, to create a spiritual exercise from the meditation on our ephemeral nature. Our ephemeral nature is moreover connected by its unavoidable umbilical cord to the inception of life in the womb. Thus it is that in the Judeo-Christian tradition in particular, and perhaps through the memory of long-forgotten faiths of earlier periods, the inevitability of death is closely linked to woman.

Our fear of death is displaced to become a fear of woman; our dread is turned to anger against her. She must have done something awfully wrong for the whole human race to be condemned to this cycle of birth and death. She must have horribly sinned. Preoccupation with death is therefore a way of exorcizing the power of women. It has become a tradition based on dread by which means anxiety can be made salutary. It is particularly salutary for men.

Oddly enough, through that peculiar quirkiness of male logic, we are invited to consider death which is caused by woman in order to mortify the flesh and avoid thinking of woman. Woman is apparently the cause and

woman is the cure; she provides a solution to the very
problem she creates. No wonder anxiety for some is
simply created by thinking about her. No wonder that
until this day in certain cultures she is kept veiled.

And where there is dread there is also desire. Like the
earth, women have been made the embodiment of the
stable and the subversive simultaneously. Unlike everyone else on the earth they are governed by an alien
planet; they are guided by a different god. They represent security if they are wives and seditious threat if they
are not. They are that element in the human psyche
identified by myth and custom as the anarchic, the
disobedient, the unruly, and they are also defined as
more 'spiritual' and given the rather unwieldy privilege
of being inspirers, muses and whatnot. They are the one
half of the human race that is the reason for all its
mistakes, its failure in achieving the ideal. Yet for many
they are the ideal, the means to grace.

What kind of paradoxical creatures are these? How
can they be trusted? Symbolic of the complexity in man's
nature, they are the ones that must first be commanded
and controlled by force if not by seduction. Let them be
buried alive and burnt. Let them be stoned and veiled.
Let them be bound at the feet and crippled by the law.

When Ṭáhirih enters the room filled with eighty men,
many of whom are scholars and trained priests, and
when they see she is unveiled, they have to face their own
lust, their own cupidity, their own narrow-mindedness
and greed. That is why some of them leave and never
return. That is presumably why one of them slits his
throat with horror. In 'Abdu'l-Bahá's story about the
quarrelling sisters and their brother it is the fear of
exposure, of humiliation, of exploitation and of troubled

inheritance that become the veil. So long as they hide behind protestations of innocence and their indignation, so long as they conceal their machinations from the knowledge of others, so long as they delude themselves from reality within the folds of their fear, or even offer the pretence of generosity beneath its guise, wealth will bring the sisters nothing but dismay. This is presumably the reason that 'Abdu'l-Bahá takes great pains to tell us why every last farthing of that inheritance came to naught, and why, in spite of repeated offers, neither Bahá'u'lláh nor the Master accepted any of it:

> Mírzá Músá did his best to urge some of the jewels on me, but I refused. Finally he requested that I accept a single ring . . . This too I refused . . .[2]

Undaunted, Mírzá Músá turns to Bahá'u'lláh and offers

> everything he possessed: orchards, lands, estates – but was refused. Then he appointed 'ulamás of 'Iráq to intercede for him . . . [who] begged Him to accept the proffered gifts. He categorically refused.[3]

Finally, several years later Mírzá Músá once again sent the same ruby ring he had earlier offered 'Abdu'l-Bahá and this time Bahá'u'lláh ordered that the gift be accepted. It was the time of the epidemic in 'Akká and the Master sent this ring to a Bahá'í in India to be sold 'with all possible speed'[4] so that the proceeds might be expended on the sick. But even the last remnants of that inheritance continued to be a veil from the truth. 'That blessed individual', writes 'Abdu'l-Bahá with wry humour, 'never sent us a penny . . . I made no complaint. Rather, I praised God, thanking Him that out of all that wealth not a fleck of dust had settled on my robe.'[5]

So much for the veils. But what of the two sisters who chose to hang onto them? What of their fears and follies? What became of them and their hoarded wealth? What kind of lives did they lead? Were they charitable in their common poverty or did they quarrel with each other over their last third and withdraw into estrangement, each beneath a private veil? Were they generous in their prosperity or filled with the fear of losing it? What sort of people did they become as the years passed by and they had to make do with less and less, accustoming themselves by degrees of resentment, to faded gentility, to anxiety, to bread and water?

What finally was their greatest fear beneath the billowing veil? Was it poverty? Was it disgrace? Was it other people's greed? Or was it the fear of relinquishing their hold on these material things? Was it their realization that detachment was, after all, inevitable? Was their greatest fear a suspicion, deeply buried, feverishly denied, that they had missed something, they had lost something, that there was not in all their inheritance that blessed thing, that something more precious than all the jewels and carpets they had watched divided on that fateful day? Call it faith, call it a more luminous word – it was what Ṭáhirih had when she stood before the shocked assemblage and cried: 'I am the Word which the Qá'im is to utter, the Word which shall put to flight the chiefs and nobles of the earth!'[6]

Perhaps, as the years passed, the sisters realized what they wanted, though they had not known it themselves before, so swathed were they in their own veils when they came to Bahá'u'lláh with their importunate demands. They admitted at that time that the machinations of others had brought them to a terrible pass and that

Bahá'u'lláh and His wisdom and His justice were all that could save them from themselves. The court, the law, and those who masqueraded in the name of religion had all let them down:

> The Persian envoy, the judge, and the faithless mujtahids have destroyed us . . . We ourselves have been remiss and we should have sought Your protection before; in any case we come now to implore Your pardon and help.[7]

They knew a power surrounded Bahá'u'lláh but were ignorant of its meaning. They insisted on staying close to Him, though they had not recognized the Cause associated with His Name.

> We will not lift our heads from off this Threshold . . . We will seek sanctuary here in this house; we will remain here, by the door . . . until He shall deign to look into our concerns and to save us from our oppressors.[8]

Fear brought them to the threshold of Bahá'u'lláh but fear veiled them from His presence.

Veils, according to Bahá'í terminology, are those delusions that we carry around based on false assumptions or misconceptions of reality. When choices or decisions are perceived through such a delusive medium the outcome is generally dim. Neither we nor anyone else benefits and frequently great harm is done. What is alarming about this process is that we very often assume the veil without questioning its validity. You might almost imagine that there was something in us inclined towards veils, but maybe that thought too is an illusion. It is like believing that a certain state is 'natural' or 'normal' just because we have never seen an alternative to it. The most disturbing consequence of veils is that we think by their means we are avoiding choices when in fact we are giving ourselves false ones.

In a book which analyzes some of the false philosophical and moral choices that women have faced over the past several decades of feminist thought, Mary Midgley and Judith Hughes tell a story about a woman whose two sons are about to be shot during the period of the French Resistance in reprisal for anti-German activities:

> The distraught woman begged the officer in charge not to take them as her husband had recently been shot in a similar reprisal. The officer agreed to spare one, on condition that she choose which should live and which should die.[9]

The loathsomeness of this tale, according to the authors, goes far beyond the fact of innocent death or painful bereavement. 'It depends', they say, 'on the phoney element of choice which is supposed to exist, on the travesty of freedom. To give her *this* choice is to mock her freedom . . . Dazed by the old images (men) do not ask how these choices relate to the real women who have to make them now . . . Unreal choices', they conclude, 'can be made only by unreal people.'[10]

Veils, then, are unreal choices that lead us to behave like unreal people. To accept them is to become a prisoner of false premises; to impose them on others reveals how much a prisoner one is oneself. Not surprisingly, one's own veils can be rent only by oneself; they are self-delusion and require self-knowledge if they are to be removed. However well-meaning our friends, however supportive the community around us, however enlightened the society or utopian the world, we remain swathed so long as our individual will is not engaged.

There is in the symbol of the veil another less abstract fear, a cultural connotation which also leaves its traces in a Bahá'í context. The veil in Islamic countries has traditionally been associated with female exclusion. It is a woman's thing. Not only does it separate her from the power centres of society, bound to a narrow and domestic world but it also symbolizes her vulnerability to men outside her world. Her veil provides her with the appearance of unassailable virtue and protects her from lascivious and greedy eyes. The reason she wears it is because she believes the eyes must be greedy, men must be lascivious and her virtue will be assailed. The veil, therefore, summarizes all that women feel and fear in a male-dominated society.

Finally, there is a third aspect to the word, in the present context, which concerns the idea of oppression. Veils have this connotation not only because of their association with women but also because of the mental and psychological oppression they symbolize for anyone. The veil is the fear that separates us from the light, that chokes the light itself, that cloaks the mind's eye in chosen doubt instead of darkened certainty. We are both unknown to ourselves and unknowing when we are veiled. Ignorance encourages fear, even when freely chosen.

There is an illuminating sentence in 'Abdu'l-Bahá's *Memorials of the Faithful* which tells us much about fear at close quarters. In describing the character of Shams-i-Duhá He recalls the remarkable conjunction of female forces at that time in Bábí history when she and the sister of Mullá Ḥusayn and his mother all associate with

Ṭáhirih 'in close companionship' and 'occupied in teaching the Faith'.[11] It must have been a formidable group:
Shams-i-Ḍuḥá, that lion of the Cause, Qurratu'l-Ayn,
Varaqatu'l-Firdaws and her mother who is described as
'possessed [of] rare attainments and accomplishments', a
woman who like Ṭáhirih was a poet and had 'composed
many poems and eloquent elegies on the afflictions of her
sons'.[12]

One cannot help imagining what it must have been
like to have been a woman sitting in the company of
these four extraordinary creatures. The room, the
anderoun, conventional, carpeted, in the back of the house
in Baghdád amidst the family apartments, with children
crawling and crying between knees, with the samovar
bubbling in the corner. The women with their veils loose
and open about them, their hair gleaming with henna,
their bodies relaxed. Or perhaps it was summer when
they would have gathered out in the garden, under the
mulberry trees, beside the pool. Maybe they did not wear
their veils there either, for the walls were high and there
would have been no men listening, except perhaps the
half-wit who did the laundry in the kitchen quarters.
There would have been women only in the company of
these four, and how one would have marvelled at them!
Imagine listening to their eloquence, their impassioned
joy, their sense of future! They seemed impervious to the
losses they might sustain! They seemed utterly fearless
and see how radiant they were! It was a marvel, a
miracle! Even though one may not have wholly grasped
all that they were saying, about this new age, about
changes in the world, about a Revelation from God that
was going to revolutionize the affairs of men and women,
how one would have longed! One would have lingered

there in that house in Baghdád, reluctant to go home. And when one went it would have been restlessly, with undefined feelings of urgency, with a sense of impending change. And at home all the ordinary duties would have seemed so petty, so paltry compared with those words still reverberating in the heart. And how boorish the husband seemed, coming home from the marketplace, demanding instant attention, complaining that the rice was burnt. And how one wanted to tell him, 'What do you know of sacrifice? Can't you see I have more important things to think about? Don't you know this is a new age that we're living in?'

At this point, having mentioned the close companionship of these four women and their intense preoccupation teaching the message of the Báb, 'Abdu'l-Bahá writes: 'Since this was in the early days of the Cause, the people were not yet afraid of it.'[13] And there one must pause and ponder. So there was a time when people were not yet afraid of it? What would have made them afraid of it? Who in particular provoked that fear? Certainly it was a fear instigated by the 'ulamá, incited by the mullás and mujtahids. But what were their reasons?

Of course the answers are many, but I am interested in the particular circumstance of that woman whose husband was annoyed. His dinner was late and the rice was spoiled and this chit of a woman he has recently married, a curse be upon her kinsmen, is standing there in the hearing of the servants and answering him back in that impertinent manner! Where has she been learning all this wisdom from, he'd like to know, sarcastically? And where has she spent the whole day that the servants have taken over the house in this disgraceful manner? What more important things has she to think about when she

doesn't even know her duties to him? Who has been
filling her head with all this nonsense? Sacrifice? He'll
teach her a thing or two about sacrifice! And naturally he
roars out of the house in a black rage and spends the
afternoon – when he would normally be snoring in a
siesta – drinking 'araq and black coffee with some of his
cronies. The world's turning topsy-turvy, he grumbles.
The next thing we know it'll be women in the marketplace. Oh yes, they agree, that's what'll happen. Have
you heard what the priest's been saying about these
awful Bábís? That's what they're wanting, I reckon,
water in the 'araq and women in the marketplace. It's a
disgrace. And the seeds of fear are planted.

The potential threat posed by the teachings of the Báb
to the power of the 'ulamá was one thing. They were
outraged by what they considered the blasphemies of this
upstart youth who took it upon himself, apparently
illiterate and unschooled as he was, to assume divine
authority over men like themselves who had spent their
lives in laboured scholarship. But the threat to their
scholastic authority, to their role as spiritual leaders of
the community, had to be translated into a form which
could directly relate to the rage of merchants in the
marketplace, to the fear of women in the streets. The
merchants and their wives were vulnerable to much
more basic threats. It was the subversion of social norms,
the reversal of time-honoured customs, the questioning
of issues most private and most inarticulate that must
have roused them to such a fury in the marketplace, to
such a blood-thirsty roar in the streets.

Ṭáhirih was the daughter of a mullá, and due to her
extraordinary intellectual abilities, had earned herself
the education of a priest; but she was a woman, and it is

this conjunction between women and fear touched upon earlier that we must finally explore. The fact of Ṭáhirih's femininity could never have been far from people's thoughts at Badasht. It would have been difficult for men of such a time and place, with their background and education, trained as so many were to become priests, to have totally ignored her sex in revering her knowledge. Many indeed chose not to revere her knowledge because of her sex. Even if a number of them succeeded in abstracting her totally into a myth – 'the very incarnation of Fáṭimih' – her face was a sufficient symbol, within the Islamic tradition, of her sexuality. Small wonder then that some of those present 's'enveloppèrent la tête de leur vêtement pour ne point voir le visage de son Altesse la Pure'.[14]

No doubt, therefore, a large percentage of that audience, unaware of the immense spiritual significance of the One in Whose presence they were sitting, uncertain even in retrospect perhaps that the episode might have been 'a God-sent test designed to separate the true from the false and distinguish the faithful from the disloyal',[15] saw the confrontation between Quddús and Ṭáhirih primarily on sexual grounds. Should Quddús refuse to submit to the request of a woman because she was his inferior? Could a woman possessed of such immense spiritual powers be a man's superior? For some present, Quddús would have been perfectly justified in the rudeness of his reply, the arrogance of his refusal, simply because of his sexual superiority. Even the implicit violence written across his face at Ṭáhirih's cataclysmic entrance – 'holding the unsheathed sword in his hand, his face betraying a feeling of inexpressible anger . . . as if he were waiting for the moment when he could strike his fatal blow at Ṭáhirih'[16] – seems to reverberate with this implied sexual outrage, a violence that in psychological terms is rooted in the threat of castration, the impulse to punish by rape.

We cannot underestimate the sexual impact of this confrontation or ignore the flood of intense and pent-up sexual emotions that surge within this episode. We should not too hastily push its significance into dimly understood abstractions or adopt Shoghi Effendi's terminology without recognizing its roots. None of the issues he raises – the 'departure from the time-honoured traditions', the 'revolution in . . . outlook, habits, ceremonials and manner of worship'[17] – can be fully grasped if we try to dilute the basic challenge posed by the principle of sexual equality in this context. It was not Ṭáhirih's station only, nor her action merely, not even her words that caused the consternation: it was her body. It is one thing to accept the concept of equality as a theory; it is quite another to be told what to think by that female body, by someone like your wife or your mother or your sister. The profound threat which this imposes on men, the fear it incites which has its roots in some earlier time, some deeper and subconscious issues, all add fuel to the fires of fanaticism that raged about the Bábí community. The women too would fear such ideas with equal if not more virulent ferocity. They would cling to their veils and revile their sisters who did not, because by their antagonism they could prove their faithfulness to the old law thereby earning honour, as Delilah did, from the priests. The veil was, finally, the symbol of sexual fear. That 'little curtain of flesh', as Blake has called the body, has become in religious traditions of the past one of the greatest impediments to the development of the soul.

I began this section with the story of the sisters, hanging on for dear life to their veils. It ends with the admission that their brother was just as much an accomplice in the tale. Their father's death and all that it symbolizes was a challenge none of them could face unveiled. How might it have been different? What might have given those young women and their brother the strength to face death, realize detachment and be free of fear?

They had been born perhaps in Persia and had come to Baghdád as small children when their father fled from the greed of the Sháh. Had they been born in 'Iráq, thirty years earlier, they might have been among the little babies tumbling at the feet of Ṭáhirih in the house of the Muftí of that city. No doubt more fuss would have been made of the little boy than the other two, who, it would have been noted, weren't all that pretty and who were rather bad-tempered too. They might have been held, briefly, in the lap of Shams-i-Ḍuḥá as she spoke with fervency about the new Faith she had espoused. They might have been offered sweetmeats and told to hush up and stop their squalling as the chanting of verses began and that beautiful voice rose in the midst of the women, spontaneous and unpremeditated. Ṭáhirih's address at the conference of Badasht was also spontaneous and unpremeditated, Shoghi Effendi tells us, but her words require the meditation of centuries:

I am the Word which the Qá'im is to utter, the Word which shall put to flight the chiefs and nobles of the earth![18]

It might be useful one last time to consider the stirring

call of this 'trumpeter' as Shoghi Effendi calls her, 'the
noblest of her sex [whose] call . . . was the death-knell of
the twelve hundred year old law of Islám'.[19] Here she is,
a woman, claiming to be that immaculate, hitherto all-
male Word 'which the Qá'im is to utter'. She is claiming
to be the Word that has been associated with the station
of the Son of God whose interpretation has depended on
those lesser sons of God, the priests. She is claiming to be
everything which in past dispensations has been associated with patriarchy: the symbol of God's Revelation,
God's Word and God's Law. She foreshadows in her
claim what 'Abdu'l-Bahá later affirmed about the
significance of the woman in the Revelation of St John,
the woman 'who fled into the wilderness, and the great
wonder appearing in the heavens – that woman clothed
with the sun, with the moon under her feet'. 'What is
meant by the woman', 'Abdu'l-Bahá states, 'is the Law
of God. For according to the terminology of the Holy
Books, this reference is to the Law, the woman being its
symbol here.'[20]

It is an earth-shattering claim. If she is the Word, and
the Qá'im is to utter it, is not her expression and her
defiance of the old order, her unrestraint and courage in
embracing the new, the very message of the age? In what
way, then, does this message challenge the men and
women that hear it? How are we to take up that call
without falling foul of the old forms of priestcraft,
without slipping into fundamentalist habits of mind,
without failing to perceive within and around all that we
do the presence of the potent King? How are we to
distinguish between the profound spiritual revolution
which this announcement has quietly ushered into our
world and the patterns of rebellion against all authority

figures to which our world has become accustomed and to a large degree inured?

The two sisters and their spoilt little brother did not have the chance to grow up free of those constricting habits of mind. The question is, what are the constricting habits with which we, the rebellious generation, have grown up? What is the nature of our freedom?

6

Freedom

For the past two hundred and fifty years, ever since Rousseau brought it to our attention that man is born free, we have been chafing against the chains in which we find ourselves. In fact, the philosophy underlying Western liberal democracy rests on the assumption that freedom is right and chains are wrong, that freedom is God-given and chains are man-made, that freedom is that blissful state achieved after political, religious, economic or psychological chains have been rent asunder. This argument has also been reversed, but its basic message has remained the same. It is the chains, according to this reversed argument, which are imposed by God, by church, by state, by school and by parents, in fact by all institutions whose authority has been questioned over the last century and a half, while freedom belongs to the assertive will, is the birthright and characteristic of the individual, must be seized and claimed and at all costs protected against interference by 'the establishment'.

The manifestos of all revolutionaries are the same. Like the message at the heart of all religions, they strike at essentially spiritual matters; we hear that immaculate 'A' ringing out of the tuning fork of our souls and we are immediately hooked. Of course freedom is our right! Of course no power on earth can have authority over the individual conscience! Of course oppression must stop and evil must be purged and equality must reign and the earth be transformed into a paradise! Of course!

But at the heart of all such revolutions there is a fear of sameness that the inward spirit of the revolutionary balks at and rejects. Haven't these cries been heard before, these tedious demands? Hasn't this pattern repeated itself and what is therefore new about it this time? What is different?

The habits of mind which produced this model of thinking, according to a recent letter of the Universal House of Justice, have emerged from a period of history 'dominated by the surging energy, the rebellious spirit and frenetic activity of adolescence'.[1] Like adolescents we are likely to discover that our revolution has not changed the habits of mind against which we have been pitting our frustrations. We have merely substituted one creed for another, one set for priests for another. We have exchanged one kind of fundamentalism for another equally fatal kind. The revolutions we keep spawning remain superficial. They affect the outer forms and structures of our behaviour and do not change the spiritual perceptions within.

It has only been in the last decade or so in the West, at least, that we have been able to see to what conclusions our logic of absolute freedom is leading. It has only been since the 'Jewish problem', as it was called in the early 1900s, has become the 'Palestinian problem' involving the whole of the Middle East, since the 'greenhouse effect' has become more threatening than the Cold War between the eastern and western blocs, since economic and environmental devastation has penetrated areas where armies and ideologies were ineffectual, since terrorism, drug warfare and AIDS have superseded the dread of a nuclear catastrophe that we have been forced to consider some of our inherited assumptions about the nature of freedom. It may be finally dawning on us that revolution is actually the most unrevolutionary solution to human problems, that the really significant revolution in human affairs would be to redefine the word itself, to interpret concepts such as freedom and individual rights in a new rather than the same old context.

In a letter sent in December 1988 to the American Bahá'ís, the Universal House of Justice expressed this need for a new context: 'Bahá'u'lláh's assertions clearly call for an examination of current assumptions.'[2] Thereafter, and throughout the ensuing letter, the House of Justice 'pauses to reflect' with us on these issues by means of some of the most soul-searching questions. It asks us to think about freedom of speech. It questions the difference between licence and liberty. It challenges us with the unanswerable debate surrounding the rights of the individual and the responsibilities of institutions. It requires that we begin to think critically.

'Should liberty be as free as is supposed in contemporary Western thought?' it asks us searchingly. 'Where does freedom limit our possibilities for progress, and where do limits free us to thrive? What are the limits', it insists, 'to the expansion of freedom [and] . . . what are the latitudes of freedom in the Bahá'í community?' When it turns its attention to the models of social order in the world today, it stimulates even more questions. It draws our attention to the fact that these models were 'in many instances, conceived in rebellion and retain the characteristics of the revolutions peculiar to an adolescent, albeit necessary, period in the evolution of human society.' And it encourages us to re-examine these

essentially adolescent roots by asking us 'What . . . was
the nature of society that gave rise to such characteristics
and such philosophies? Where have these taken mankind?
Has their employment satisfied the needs and expectations of the human spirit?'[3]

These are immense questions. Each one deserves a
book to consider. The reason I draw on them now is not
to do them justice but to lean on them, draw sustenance
from them, and discover in them the principles by which,
once more, we might understand ourselves in the mirror
of Bahá'í history. The historical reaction I want to
explore in this essay concerns that of the adolescent, the
rebel. Since we are collectively emerging from a period of
adolescence it might be illuminating to look at one
particular youth in Bahá'í history who is remarkable for
his rebellious nature and explore, in the light of this
important letter from the House of Justice about
freedom, his response to Bahá'u'lláh's 'call for an
examination of current assumptions'. I would like to look
at the story of Badí', therefore, in relation to questions
about liberty of spirit, freedom of self-expression and the
laws of man and God.

The first time we have occasion to meet Badí' is recorded
by Nabíl in his unpublished works and affords us a
personal and familiar glimpse of a youth for whom
questions of freedom and self-restraint are as yet
unresolved. Nabíl has been instructed by Bahá'u'lláh to
travel through Persia strengthening the believers in the
Covenant. It is one of the several occasions, as 'Abdu'l-
Bahá describes in *Memorials of the Faithful*, when Nabíl,
who longs to be in the presence of Bahá'u'lláh, is
instructed by Him to travel and inspire the friends in

Persia. In fact, the whole of Nabíl's own history seems to be tense with the conflict between desire for freedom and demand for obedience. Repeatedly he returns to the presence of Bahá'u'lláh, whether in Baghdád or Constantinople or Adrianople, consumed with love and longing, only to be instructed by Him to travel again back to Persia. On this particular occasion, as 'Abdu'l-Bahá notes, he was 'given specific orders to travel everywhere, and in every region to raise the call that God was now made manifest: to spread the blissful tidings that the Sun of Truth had risen'.[4] And he came to Níshápúr.

Here he was entertained at the home of one of the believers, Ḥájí 'Abdu'l-Majíd-i-Níshápúrí, who had a seventeen-year-old son called Áqá Buzurg. The domestic arrangements between father and son, however, cause Nabíl considerable embarrassment. He finds to his surprise that the father is performing those tasks that should normally have been undertaken by the son. The menial tasks of service, providing water for ablutions, providing tea and other refreshments, would normally be performed by the women of the household but, as Adib Taherzadeh points out, 'it was against the custom of the time for the female members of the family to entertain guests of the opposite sex'.[5] Nabíl would therefore have expected, as a matter of common courtesy, that any son in the household would have undertaken such tasks and it was a mark of great disrespect that his father should have to serve the guests personally. Áqá Buzurg, however, clearly had no interest in assuming the role either of a servant or of a woman. He was determined to overthrow all such old-fashioned conventions. He was nowhere to be seen.

'Do you not have a grown-up son?' inquires Nabíl, somewhat amazed.

Hájí 'Abdu'l-Majíd assents, adding with a sigh that 'he was not obedient to him.'[6]

'Call him to me,' says Nabíl. 'Let me see him.'

It is at this point that the tall, awkward youth enters the story: a dramatic entrance because clearly a reluctant one. By a masterful stroke of genius, the poet and the historian combine with the instinctive dramatist in Nabíl. Nothing could be more immediately comic and more potentially powerful than this scene, in which Nabíl sits and exhorts the father while the son stands by, a most unwilling eavesdropper.

If Áqá Buzurg had been vociferous about not wishing to take the female role of subservience, he was even less inclined to hang around while his father entertained yet another boring Bahá'í. The words of the Universal House of Justice are very appropriate here, when it describes the adolescent characteristics as 'conspicuous ... in ... inordinate scepticism, ... and grudging respect'.[7] He was, as Mr Taherzadeh observes with some detachment, 'not touched sufficiently by the spirit of the Faith' to make him in any way interested in meeting such people. Through the lines we can read a little of the remoteness and estrangement of spirit here, the rejecting and rebellious nature. He remained, says Mr Taherzadeh quietly, 'cold and aloof' to the glory of the Cause.[8]

What glory? In the company of a bunch of sycophantic merchants and timid shopkeepers? What glory was there in sidling along the alleyways, anxious not to be observed, on the way to some Bahá'í gathering? What glory in huddling together inside the modest home of some insignificant carpet dealer in order to listen to heavy sighs and sometimes weeping at the difficulties of the times, the hardships, yes, oh dear, the shaking of heads over the hardships! They were like a bunch of old women, these Bahá'ís, with their endlessly long readings filled with incomprehensible words in Arabic and their mute acceptance of persecution. He wanted none of it, not he! He was a wild young colt, straining at the leash, eager to bend his strength against the odds. He wasn't interested in any of this submissive nonsense.

And so he stood there, by the doorway, fuming, having brought in the basin for the stranger to wash his travel-stained hands. And he stood there chafing to be gone, and shifting from foot to foot, waiting for his father's nod to summon in the samovar. And he stood there, stifling yawns, as these two old men droned on and on about this and that, and all of it Bahá'í stuff, naturally. What else *could* they talk about? God! It was so boring . . .

And what did they talk about?

We may not know exactly, from Nabíl's records, but we can probably make a fair guess. It was sometime in 1867 or 1868, just about the time when Bahá'u'lláh was, from Adrianople, sending His cataclysmic letters to the kings, the first act of public proclamation of the Cause. It was at a time, too, when the machinations of Mírzá Yaḥyá had become so overt, so nefarious and so flagrant that the hand of Bahá'u'lláh had been caused to shake through the effects of the poison ministered by His half-brother. It was a time when the narrow, secret world of the Bahá'ís was being challenged by a summoning from their Lord to see their task as world-embracing and revolutionary.

Áqá Buzurg was all for revolutions. He had dimly heard of the early Bábís, and may have even known, in a detached kind of way, about Ṭáhirih and Quddús, Mullá Ḥusayn and Ḥujjat, Vaḥíd and others. But these heroic men and women belonged to the generation before his and their contemporaries were far too timid to inspire much more than contempt, leave alone revolution. Now here was a man, this traveller, whom he had to admit did have some fire in his eyes, some eloquence to his tongue. He'd looked like any other old Bahá'í at first, full of reverence and prayers, deference and piety. The sullen boy sulking by the door couldn't abide the timorous piety of old men. But when he started to talk you realized that here was a man who had actually lived and met these early heroes. He was a man who knew them. Áqá Buzurg's curiosity was piqued at last.

From 'Abdu'l-Bahá's description of Nabíl on this journey through Persia, it is not hard to imagine how the young man, leaning against the door jamb, may have gradually been drawn, against his will, to actually listen to what was being said. It is not hard to imagine him, between the serving of tea and the bringing in of the rice and sauces, becoming so engrossed that only his father's peremptory cough would have reminded him that the time had come for the clearing of the plates. It is not hard to imagine his reluctance, almost, to leave the room to bring in the fruit and the sweetmeats and the interminable tea, again, in case he should miss what was being said next. Nabíl, writes 'Abdu'l-Bahá, 'was truly on fire, driven by restive love. With great fervour he would pass through a country, bringing this best of messages and reviving the hearts. He flamed like a torch in every company, he was the star of every assemblage, to all who came he held out the intoxicating cup. He journeyed as to the beat of drums . . .'[9]

The blood in the veins of that listening youth must
have begun to beat with the same pulse. With every
sentence Nabíl drew his audience closer to the One he
called his Best-Beloved. With every thought he circled in
adoration round the Blessed Beauty. Bahá'u'lláh! may
my life and soul be offered as a sacrifice to His very
Name! Bahá'u'lláh! through whom the kings and rulers
of the earth shall be made to tremble and through whose
very breath the civilizations of the earth will be shaken
asunder! Bahá'u'lláh! in obedience to whose command a
new world order is now at this very hour being unfurled,
and in whose grasp lie the reins of all creation, the future
of all civilization! Oh, Bahá'u'lláh! Bahá'u'lláh!

Finally, with the lighting of the lamp as evening drew
in, it is not hard to imagine how Nabíl might have
beckoned the now intensely attentive youth to step inside
and be seated with them, there, with his hands placed
respectfully on his knees, palms upward and open, to
hear the recitation of a Tablet from the hand of
Bahá'u'lláh Himself. It is not hard to conceive of that
young man's state of mind and heart as the wondrous
words were intoned in the glimmering room, with the
lamp casting strange shadows on the ceiling, with the
sound of the nightingale drifting in through the window
and the dark moths fluttering:

> Release yourselves, O nightingales of God, from the
> thorns and brambles of wretchedness and misery, and
> wing your flight to the rose-garden of unfading
> splendour. O My friends that dwell upon the dust!
> Haste forth unto your celestial habitation. Announce
> unto yourselves the joyful tidings: 'He Who is the Best-
> Beloved is come! He hath crowned Himself with the
> glory of God's Revelation, and hath unlocked to the

face of men the doors of His ancient Paradise.' Let all eyes rejoice, and let every ear be gladdened, for now is the time to gaze on His beauty, now is the fit time to hearken to His voice.[10]

But whatever is happening to the boy? What's the matter with him? He's fallen face down on the carpet, prostrated! There's a terrible noise coming from his throat! Good God! Is the child weeping?

And Hájí 'Abdu'l-Majíd would have wanted to come forward to his son, perhaps, to lift his tear-stained face from the floor, had Nabíl not restrained him. He would have sensed the youth's pride, and only after the boy had staggered to his feet and fled, sobbing, from the room would that powerful voice have lifted in chanting once more. And from his room at the far end of the house, Áqá Buzurg, who would be renamed Badí' by Bahá'u'lláh, would have heard it and have been overwhelmed anew.

He wept throughout that night, we are told, a young man of whom his father said 'I have never heard him weep before'. And it was a changed being who stood there by the door pale and ready to serve tea to the guest in the morning. After he left the house to conduct some affairs in the town his father told Nabíl, 'I am prepared to serve him if he remains steadfast in the Cause.'

Now Badí' had one consuming desire: to meet Bahá'u'lláh face to face, to be honoured by attaining His presence. He was determined that his father should permit him to accompany Nabíl on the remainder of his journey, to stay with him until he returned to the presence of Bahá'u'lláh. But now it was his zeal rather than his resentment that had to be curbed. Not before he had finished his studies, insisted his father. Not before he had prepared himself for such an honour by studying the whole of the *Kitáb-i-Íqán*. Not before he had actually copied that entire book in his own hand would he be granted his freedom.

As the Universal House of Justice so succinctly states: 'any constructive view of freedom implies limits'.[11] For Badí' the meaning of freedom was already beginning to change shape; its structure was shifting in conformity with the Covenant. Freedom could no longer be divorced from obedience. For how could he chafe now or be impatient when the task at hand was to immerse himself in the words of the One Whom he had set his heart upon meeting? What was the use of freedom to him if he could not use it to obey his Lord? When he was ready to leave his father fussed about, acquiring goods to sustain him on the journey, arranging for companions to accompany him along the way and a mule to carry him there. But Badí' had begun the journey of his heart already. His body only had to catch up with his soul that was already on its way, marching ahead to the beat of drums. When he reached Yazd he parted company with his companion, gave him all his possessions and proceeded towards Baghdád on foot.

It was to be a long and arduous journey. He walked from Yazd to Baghdád, from Baghdád to Mosul, and finally, when news came of Bahá'u'lláh's exile to 'Akká, he turned his face towards the Holy Land and began to walk towards that prison city, reaching the studded land gate, crowded with beggars, crammed with travellers and watched by the hawk-eyed enemies of Bahá'u'lláh we are told, some time in early 1869.

The rest of the story is known well enough and is full of unspoken mysteries: how he attained the presence of

Bahá'u'lláh on two occasions and was ushered into His presence utterly alone, with no witnesses, no one to hear the words that were exchanged; how he was told by Bahá'u'lláh to proceed to Haifa and there await his instructions and the precious case containing the Tablet to the Sháh which he had been elected to deliver; how he was cautioned to speak to no one, associate with no one along the way back to Persia, and how he obeyed. How joyously he obeyed! How finally, after that bleak and ecstatic journey which took about four months to complete on foot, he was seen by the king himself on his hunting expedition, a strange figure, robed in white, and sitting on a rock for three days together. How he was brought before the king at his own adamant insistence. How, once there, he solemnly handed him the precious letter, crying out the words Bahá'u'lláh had told him to utter: 'O King, I have come unto thee from Sheba with a weighty message.'[12]

The story of Badí' moves us for many reasons. There is scarcely another single martyrdom that is so closely documented as his, that describes in such chilling detail the degrees of torture he endured, that covers to the last gory moment the catalogue of his physical anguish. But it is not so much what he endures physically as the spirit in which he endures it which haunts us. It is that spirit which I think is invoked by the letter of the Universal House of Justice to which I have been referring in this essay. This letter seems to carry the spirit of Badí' to the West, to remind us, in our 'confusion of attitudes', of his singleness of purpose, the miracle of his transformation, the meaning of his freedom. By linking history to this letter I would like to suggest that Badí' himself might be a messenger to our hearts, showing us by his precise interpretation and immaculate response to Bahá'u'lláh, what there is about the nature and the implementation of freedom that would enable us, too, to carry the Bahá'í message to the kings and rulers of the world.

We cannot dwell on what took place in those two interviews which Badí' had with Bahá'u'lláh; they constitute the innermost response of each one of us to this Cause. Such communion may not be guessed. But we can observe Badí''s outward response, and it may tell us of those mysteries. Only by our actions can a spiritual revolution be dimly gauged, and even then, only with awe. The efficacy of institutional and individual behaviour, states the House of Justice, depends less on the imposition of outward restraints than on the inner motions of the spirit. The pattern depends 'not so much on the force of law, which admittedly must be respected, as on the recognition of a mutuality of benefits, and on the spirit of cooperation maintained by the willingness, the courage, the sense of responsibility, and the initiative of individuals'. These inner motivations, moreover, are 'expressions of . . . devotion and submission to the will of God'.[13]

It would be impossible to understand Badí' without affirming these inner motives, without realizing that his actions rest unequivocally, first and foremost, on his 'recognition of the sovereignty of God and [his] submission to His will' which, according to the Universal House of Justice, is the only vantage point that gives us the correct perspective on 'such fundamental issues as individual rights and freedom of expression'.[14] The vehicle for the practical fulfilment of our recognition of God's will is the Covenant, and the instrument through which that Covenant affects the affairs of men is the

Administrative Order. The distinctive nature of this Order, the fact that there can be no comparison between it and 'the diverse systems which the minds of men, at various periods of their history, have contrived for the government of human institutions'[15] is symbolized, for the present purposes, by the way in which Badí' puts into action the injunctions of Bahá'u'lláh.

Bahá'u'lláh had told him to travel alone, to mix with no one along the way, and to mingle with none of the Bahá'ís when he arrived in Persia. His determination to obey this injunction is enacted to a literal degree and it is only through haunting glimpses of Badí' seen by his bemused fellow-travellers walking about a hundred feet from the road that we know anything of his long hard journey from Palestine to Ṭihrán. By his attitude we are reminded of the non-imitative and entirely distinctive nature of the Administrative Order, 'a departure both in origin and concept'[16] from any of the existing systems of the past. By maintaining this separation between himself and his fellow-travellers, Badí', that young radical, symbolizes the absolute independence of the Administrative Order, 'for notwithstanding its inclination to democratic methods'[17] this Order treads a different path. Western democracies may believe that the individual has certain rights and freedoms, that an individual should be protected from totalitarian extremes and tyrannical practices, and it may be true to say that in some ways this goal is shared by the Bahá'ís; but the path we follow, like that taken by Badí', must be unique. Badí''s spiritual freedom was distinguished literally by his physical distance from the other travellers, a distance, stressed repeatedly in the letter of the House of Justice, between licence and liberty, between Western definitions of

freedom and 'freedom to unite, freedom to progress,
freedom in peace and joy'.[18]

It is significant, however, that although Badí' maintained his distance, we still have some record of those on
the journey who did have occasion to exchange a few
words with him. The spiritual distance which preserves
his inner freedom does not make him inaccessible to his
travelling companions who find him 'a very happy
person, smiling, patient, thankful, gentle and humble'.[19]
How astonishing to hear such epithets applied to the
erstwhile rebel, the sullen boy by the doorway! How
much stranger still to associate them with the chastened
figure we later see on the rock of arrival, his lips sealed,
in a state of fasting and prayer! Who can forget his
vulnerability there, his exposure? The Universal House
of Justice commenting on the importance of the Bahá'í
review procedures and the danger of relaxing all restraints
just as the Faith is emerging from obscurity might just as
well have been referring to those extraordinary circumstances. Though it is speaking to us in the West, the
words in its letter recall this passionate and intense
young man in the East over a hundred years ago, seated
on the high rock, dressed in white robes, awaiting the
attention of the king:

> The Faith is as yet in its infancy. Despite its emergence
> from obscurity, even now the vast majority of the
> human race remains ignorant of its existence; more-
> over, the vast majority of its adherents are relatively
> new Bahá'ís. The change implied by this new stage in
> its evolution is that whereas heretofore this tender
> plant was protected in its obscurity from the attention
> of external elements, it has now become exposed. This

exposure invites close observation, and that observation will eventually lead to opposition . . .[20]

Badí''s exposure was duly observed and, as we know, it was an observation which led directly to opposition. But without straining the comparison in such a way that would suggest our efforts to proclaim the Cause are quite as spiritually dramatic or historically important, it is nevertheless useful to see the similarity between his state of mind as he sat there on his rock and our own as we sit on Assemblies or with our own creative thoughts. What was going on in the mind of the boy who was fasting, praying and waiting? What thoughts must have occurred to him, knowing how much depended on the words he was about to utter? He had, like the proverbial nightingale, to deliver his clear message, but what should be the manner in which he did it? This surely was as important as the message he carried. Did he have a tongue 'matchless' enough? Did he have a spirit pure enough? Every word he uttered in his call to the Sháh was freighted with significance. No wonder he fasted; no wonder he prayed. As the House of Justice states:

> Speech is a powerful phenomenon. Its freedom is both to be extolled and feared. It calls for an acute exercise of judgement, since both the limitation of speech and the excess of it can lead to dire consequences.[21]

So much was at stake! How often, one wonders, during those three days of preparation did Badí' mull over the dire consequences for him if he addressed the Sháh. If he uttered one false word he might never get any further with his message and could be put to death on the spot, for the king was despotic. If he in any way compromised or delayed in his delivery, how could he be worthy of this great undertaking given to him by Bahá'u'lláh? How thoughtfully he must have weighed the words, how carefully he must have gauged the limits of his free expression as he sat there!

Like the letter of the House of Justice which reminds us that our ideas of liberty are not always those shared by Western democracies, Badí' not only maintained his distance from the other travellers along the caravan route of society but also kept his mission distinctive from those of thousands of petitioners who approached the Sháh with their requests. Neither the message he was carrying nor the manner in which he delivered it catered to the whims of a despotic monarch or diluted its impact in order to become more palatable to the tastes of the time. He had no intention of watering anything down, not he. He was the cup-bearer, he was the chosen messenger. No skulking in the alleys, no whispering in the shadows for him! How his heart must have leapt and danced!

But it was hardly in keeping for a petitioner to be so exultant! He should be abject; he should be grovelling. Just say it is a petition and not a letter, the guards had urged, when his awful presumption became apparent. You'll get along much better if you just use the standard form, the acceptable clichés. Don't be so stubborn, he was advised, this is the Sháh of Persia and you need to remember who you're addressing, that's all, don't be so arrogant! But Badí' was coming from the King of Kings and waited to deliver his message as an ambassador and not a beggar. Nothing could swerve him or make him compromise his standards. It's the difference between life and death, they warned him, don't be such a fool. But Badí' doggedly refused.

The 'checks and balances' referred to by the House of Justice in its letter are inward and spiritual; they are not based on any standards of men. Badí' was utterly free of the curbs and restraints current among his contemporaries, the 'hang-ups' and mental agendas among those acquainted with the court. He had spoken to no one and been influenced by none. This inner freedom of his soul was vital if his mission was to be a success. And clearly it was a success. Who can forget his laughter under the branding irons, his incomprehensible laughter, as they whipped him and branded him afresh? Who can ever forget that face set between his executioners, as he kneels in chains after the torture, in one of the few photographs of him that remain?

This portrait of Badí' facing his death is the image of him that lingers longest: a young man born bound to a rebellious nature and consenting freely to these chains of love. Unable to endure the tepid humiliations of serving guests, here he is so transformed that he has chosen to be beaten and burned by martyrdom. Impatient with the smaller and pettier conventions of parental authority, here he has learned that 'authority [was] an indispensible aspect of freedom' and committed himself to the highest authority in the world, the will of God. Death redefines the human spirit, it seems, and changes the meaning of words and their implementation. Death liberates our understanding of liberty.

7

Women

Death, that mysterious land from which no traveller returns, is the last mortal territory remaining unexplored, and we have plenty of myths about it but few maps. Individuals who have suffered and through their pain seen something veiled to diurnal eyes have left us sketches, faint glimmers on paper, but no maps. Societies have left us their beliefs and their denials, artists and poets have had visions, generals have created strategies, but none has been able to command a plain view, or describe the fording of the river, the exact dimensions of the banks on the further shore that lead to that vast plain.

Unlike death, however, women are rapidly becoming much less mysterious. Soon, with all the writing they are doing about their emotions, their mothers, their daughters, their relationship to the workplace and the legal system, they will have become quite as dull as men, and entirely unenigmatic.

There is however a kind of death with which women have been familiar in the past and remain closely associated with even now: erasure. Death by disappearance from the text of what is interesting. Death by obscurity. The 'original sin' that leads to such death has been simply the fact of one's sex. In our efforts to reclaim the significance of women in history we frequently commit the crime of elevating the flamboyant, the notorious, at the cost of minimizing the importance of their quiet sisters. In this sense too, as feminists, we may discover that death has sneaked up on us unawares. There must be ways of mapping out the unknown that do not lead to the erasure and disappearance of feminine culture.

We are accustomed, when talking about redefining roles for women, to recall pioneer figures who have explored these unknown lands, dramatic examples, characters like Ṭáhirih who have daring and eloquence and zeal. However, there are millions of us who have much less daring, hardly any eloquence and only enough zeal to put one foot in front of the other. Do we fail because, unlike Ṭáhirih, we cannot be archetypes? Are we doomed forever because our gestures cannot be elemental, our words continuously profound? Before we bury ourselves in such self-imposed obscurity it would be useful to raise the question of context.

Context, at its most simplistic, is the historical soil which gives rise to circumstances in which particular individuals are effective or not. If the soil is right it is likely that certain human reactions can take root, and we see recurring, as in the world of nature, archetypal responses in history. It is interesting in this regard to recall a refutation of the claims of the Bábís entitled *Ihqáqu'l-Ḥaqq*, in which, according to the learned mullá who compiled them, one of the thirty heresies of which this damnable sect is guilty is the 'Denial of the Resurrection and belief in Metempsychosis and the like'. Briefly, according to this heresy, Bábís, and by inference Bahá'ís too, rather than insisting on the resurrection of the body, urge the idea of ' "Return" (Raj'at) to the

life of this world of the *dramatis personae* – both believers
and unbelievers – of previous ... Dispensations ...
[I]n reality it appears that such "returns" are regarded
by Bábís less as re-incarnations than as re-manifestations
of former types, comparable to the repetition of the same
parts in a drama by fresh actors, or the re-writing of an
old story.'[1] In other words, within the spiritual context
created by a new Manifestation of God, there is a
recurrence of certain patterns in human behaviour, a
repeat performance, if you will, invoked by those special
circumstances. This particular context seems to stir
the archetypes to arise and express themselves within
us: those archetypes of loyalty or betrayal, the woman
who loves, the man who denies three times at the cock's
crow, the one who suffers silently and endures with
patience, the other who risks all and dies in a blaze of
tragedy.

What Ṭáhirih did, and how she did it, was in some
ways an example of 'metempsychosis'. She played an
immortal part in the drama of the Bábí dispensation, a
role that arose from the context of that time as well as
from her own personality and which could not have been
performed by another soul or in any other way. Not only
does her immediate historical context colour every one of
her words and actions, but we have to measure her
significance, as an individual, against a kind of metatext:
that vast backdrop of change which must affect human
society and our instincts towards each other, a change
destined to evolve 'mysteriously, slowly, and resistlessly'[2]
over the next 500,000 years of Bahá'u'lláh's dispensation.
Seen in relation to this immense, almost galactic, context
the actual gesture of standing before a crowd of men
unveiled is hardly significant at all. It is the principle of

emergence that matters. It is the quiet and repeated courage of millions of women who begin to map the uncharted territories of their lives in order to contribute to the 'ever-advancing civilization'. Only this will turn the tide of human history.

I would like to introduce two women, one from the West and one from the East, who are the quiet sisters of Ṭáhirih, whose lives may seem less remarkable and much less dramatically defined, but who provide, in their own way and within their chosen context, a response to the dilemmas of the veil quite as important as what Ṭáhirih achieves. They are both women whose silent contributions might easily be overshadowed and eclipsed unawares but who are equally important examples also of 'metempsychosis'. One was the sister of Mullá Ḥusayn, a woman whose personal name – Jinab-i-Maryam – Nabíl omitted to mention, so opaque is she, but whose title 'Varaqatu'l-Firdaws' links her, in symbolic language, with the Word of the Qá'im, the song of the Nightingale. The other is Madame Laura Clifford Barney through whose indefatigable efforts we have 'Abdu'l-Bahá's *Some Answered Questions*. The lives of both these women depend largely on the social and family contexts in which they found themselves; it was their behaviour in relation to these contexts that makes them memorable.

We are all addressed by Bahá'u'lláh as 'nightingales of God' and exhorted to free ourselves from the thorns and brambles of wretchedness and misery. We also find applied to the human heart and spirit many references to other birds, all the way from phoenixes to owls. But we cannot read of a 'nightingale of paradise' without recalling that eternal bird who has sung to the unheeding generations of the past and will sing forever and again, as long as the sovereignty of God and His domain will endure. The nightingale, moreover, is no common bird, and according to Persian tradition, has always sought 'the charm of the rose'. In the literary traditions of the West also it is the nightingale of 'affection and desire', pressing its soft breast against the thorn in sacrifice as it warbles melodies unseen and sweet. According to classical mythology it was, moreover, a bird associated with a woman's suffering, for Philomel who was brutally raped and had her tongue cut out was transformed, through the pity of the gods, into a nightingale. In other respects, however, it is the very commonness of this dull-looking brown bird that is conducive to its invisibility. Undiscriminating and entirely democratic, it sings its song with utter self-effacement to emperor and clown and anyone else who has ears to hear.

Bahá'u'lláh gave the title of Varaqatu'l-Firdaws, the Nightingale of Paradise, to a woman about whom we know hardly anything at all. The brief chronicle of her life does not even emerge into the main body of Nabíl's text, but lies obscure, in a thicket of references, in both French and English footnotes, devoted ostensibly to her brother Mullá Ḥusayn and her respected husband, Shaykh Abú-Turáb of Qazvín.[3] The latter, we are told, was 'a scholar and philosopher such as is rarely met with'; in this respect, too, Varaqat'ul-Firdaws differs from Ṭáhirih whose husband was a complete boor. The distinction of her brother and the rare qualities of her husband, however, serve only to erase her even more effectively from the page. When we finally reach a description of her, it is through her husband's words, for she herself remains mute. Repeatedly we hear of her silence, that 'she has never uttered a word', that 'she refrains altogether from speaking of the past', that 'she never asks for clothes or travelling-money'. So silent is she that 'no unprivileged person hath so much as heard her voice'. And yet she was called a nightingale. Her behaviour, therefore, must bear witness with an eloquence unsurpassed by words to something more than we could hear her say.

Her husband, a man of highly-refined sensibilities, tells us that when he married her three years before in Karbilá she had been 'but an indifferent scholar'. Even in her mother tongue, Persian, she did not impress him as having either much ability or potential. Now, three years later, 'she can expound texts from the Qur'án', he tells us, 'and explain the most difficult questions and the most subtle points of the doctrine of the Divine Unity'. Clearly the lady is not dumb. So remarkable are her intellectual and spiritual powers, and so commanding her eloquence when she chooses to speak, that her husband asserts, 'I have never seen a man who was her equal in this, or in the readiness of apprehension.' High praise indeed from any man. Particularly high praise from a man who was himself trained in the schools of philosophy and religious scholarship. But this man has also recognized the message of the Báb. He knows that the source of his wife's gifts and talents lies in her own dedication to the teachings of the Báb and 'through converse with her holiness the Pure', i.e. Ṭáhirih. He himself has such a love and devotion towards the Báb that 'if anyone did so much as mention the name of His Supreme Holiness . . . he could not restrain his tears'.

There is a curious intermingling of masculine and feminine roles in this couple: he weeps and she reads.

It was hardly your run-of-the-mill marriage by mid-nineteenth century standards anywhere, leave alone Persia. During the three brief years of this marriage, years corresponding to the most turbulent period of Bábí history, years of sacrifice and deprivation, martyrdom and persecution, Shaykh Abú-Turáb says of his wife: 'I have seen in her a patience and resignation rare even in the most self-denying men.' Although, to his profound shame and unease, he has been unable to send her 'a single dínár' during this difficult period, she has neither complained nor grumbled, though 'she has supported herself only with the greatest difficulty'. Not only is her conversation entirely free of blame and recrimination but, he tells us, in spite of having 'literally nothing to put on save the one well-worn dress which she wears', she asks neither for clothes nor travel money 'but ever seeks reasonable excuses wherewith to set me at my ease and prevent me from feeling ashamed'.

It has become a common theme of feminist studies that women need to recognize the force of patriarchal expectation placed on them which requires obedience and silence, submission and patience under all conditions. It has become a cliché of the liberation movement that we need to reclaim our voices and our bodies if we are to reclaim our rights as women. In the light of such common themes, such current clichés, the life of Varaqatu'l-Firdaws could be just one more story of a suppressed woman. Her silence could be interpreted not as chosen but imposed; the praise given to her qualities of 'purity, chastity and virtue' could be interpreted as a travesty of justice. The price of being an ideal wife would, it could easily be assumed, have been extorted at the enormous cost of her personality, her individuality. Who is she really, after all, but a figment of some male fantasy? Her sheer absence of story is the most damning evidence of our failure, as Bahá'ís, to live according to the ideal of equality.

At this point it would be useful to remind ourselves of context. Not only is there the context of the chronicler himself, a man who began life as a shepherd in Zarand with, as he himself acknowledges, 'a most rudimentary education',[4] but also the larger social context of Persia in the mid-nineteenth century, a country and people dominated by a corrupt court and influenced by an over-weening Shí'ih clergy. Within such a context of chauvinist politics, scholarship and theology why should women be a fit subject for history or philosophy? The pages of Nabíl's *Dawn-Breakers* are filled with countless women. They ride beside their husbands and sacrifice their children. They are humiliated, beaten and raped. They are paraded on horseback as the heads of their sons and husbands are held aloft on pikes. They carry stones and build forts; they cut off their hair and use it to bind together the fracturing guns at Nayríz. They were no doubt among those who helped grind the bones of dead horses and who rushed out under cannon fire to gather the new grass to eat at Fort Shaykh Ṭabarsí. But they have no names and Nabíl does not go out of his way to mention them. Here and there a woman with a name emerges, a Zaynab, a Varaqatu'l-Firdaws, but there must have been countless others whom he did not mention. Is there really any point in asking why? Aren't all the hundreds of reports currently being written about female mortality rates, malnutrition statistics, labour and health problems among Third World women a sufficient proof that answers to such questions will require several more generations of questions being asked?

Furthermore, there is the specific context of the particular life of this quiet woman who has disappointed the feminist in us by being so different from Ṭáhirih. She is a woman who was a close companion to the dynamic Qurratu'l-'Ayn. She was the student of one of the most forceful and self-assertive women of her age. And she is evidently not stupid. Her ability to absorb, to learn once there is the chance to do so, her readiness, as her husband puts it, of 'apprehension' as well as comprehension, are acute. She could certainly have assimilated the forthright courage of her teacher, and was quite eloquent enough to have emulated her on more than one occasion. But why did she choose to withhold her powers? Why was she so invisible? Why did she find excuses for her husband and acquiesce so readily to her brother?

Even by feminist standards, however, the silence and submission of Varaqatu'l-Firdaws is not stereotypical. Her husband is no tyrant under whose cruel injustice she bows down with Griselda-like patience. On the contrary, he is a man whose sensitivities seem 'feminine' according to such suspect stereotypes. His appreciation of her is the only remaining testimony we have of her life and his personal sacrifices are at least as intense as hers. It is significant that she holds her tongue on money matters but certainly speaks up when it comes to expounding, explaining and proving the truth in which she so ardently believes. Her silence is due neither to fear of punishment nor desire for approval. Clearly any punishment she might receive from a husband pales to insignificance before the persecutions she is prepared to accept at the hands of a fanatical clergy. And any approval he might give her is secondary before the good-pleasure of God, to Whom she has dedicated her life.

When one considers how easy it would be to ignore the context which surrounds the silence of Varaqatu'l-Firdaws, death by erasure or misconception becomes inevitable. It is precisely to save us from that kind of death that the Manifestations of God bring us Their messages, time and again. It is in order that we recognize the vast metatext in which our smaller context of individual life has been cast. It is that we might grasp the relationship between the lesser and the greater Covenants, a vitally important 'heresy'! It is so we can remember, rather than ignore.

In the *Kitáb-i-Íqán* Bahá'u'lláh identifies one of the major reasons why the truth of every Divine Revelation is so frequently ignored. 'The wayward of every age', He states, 'have failed to fathom the deeper import of these weighty and pregnant utterances, and imagined the answer of the Prophets of God to be irrelevant to the questions they asked them ...'[5] Failure to see the connection between question and answer is tantamount to a failure to penetrate the surface and recognize deeper meanings which in turn is similar to ignoring the context of a word or act. Why there need be such a breakdown, however, requires further probing. What causes us to miss the relevance and the context and be blind to what Bahá'u'lláh interestingly terms 'pregnant utterances'? The metaphor, besides being distinctly feminine and permitting thereby a correspondence between being misunderstood, mistaken and misjudged and being a woman, also contains the suggestion of organic growth, hidden vitality and faith in time. Pregnancy is a state that is often mysterious even to the woman herself who is experiencing it. To judge it merely by externals is to entirely miss the dynamism it contains.

It is remarkable that Bahá'u'lláh should invite us to become so intimately acquainted with a process so peculiarly feminine when we attempt to probe the meaning of His 'weighty and pregnant utterances'. Might there be a further suggestion that mankind's failure to make connections between its own questions and the answers revealed by God is linked, by analogy, to a similar failure to grasp the significance of women and their necessary contribution to the world? Could this analogy, furthermore, persuade us to reassess what we consider 'significant' in history, to explore the drama from a fresh perspective, with new actors, to marvel at the old story rewritten? It may be due to the breakdown we so frequently experience between questions and answers that the lives of women such as Varaqatu'l-Firdaws seem 'irrelevant', their story dull, their drama disappointing.

There is a curious Tablet revealed by 'Abdu'l-Bahá which seems to be an exercise in making connections and learning the links between question and answer.[6] It is addressed to 'O thou who hast eyes to see' and proceeds to connect a series of apparently unrelated analogies: bud and perfume, herb and fruit, pages of a book and the meaning of words written on them, and finally, the good old foetus in the womb of immortality. True scholars, which I am not, will no doubt in the future explore the full context of this Tablet and discover reasons, perhaps, for 'Abdu'l-Bahá's references here. What, for instance, has been witnessed by the 'one who hast eyes to see' and who was he or she? What was it that 'pertaineth to the realm of vision' but had mysterious connections with other worlds of meaning? What, in other words, was the literal context?

But there is a spiritual context into which this Tablet fits which is why I find it so relevant to the question of women and their erasure, to the significance of the relationship between question and answer. This is the context that we find suddenly thrust upon us with the last sentence of the Tablet quoted below in full. After the swing from bud to perfume to herb to fruit to page to word to meaning to womb to immortality 'Abdu'l-Bahá calmly concludes:

> An observant traveller passing along a way will certainly recall his discoveries to mind, unless some accident befall him and efface the memory.

It is a statement which, in the context of all that has gone before, appears at first reading to be like a thunderclap out of a clear blue sky. What journey? Which traveller? we want to ask. But He's gone. The Tablet is ended. So we go back to the beginning and read it through once more, alert this time for the thunderbolt. And it comes.

> An observant traveller passing along a way will certainly recall his discoveries to mind, unless some accident befall him and efface the memory.

The sentence demands a response from the reader that challenges him to see the whole Tablet as a journey passed, that requires him to judge his own powers of observation during the journey. Can we call ourselves observant readers or are we merely 'wayward' travellers? Can we recall the discoveries, be attuned to the connections or has some accident effaced the memory? Might we become true explorers, then, and map out the wonders of this journey on the tablets of our hearts where they can never be effaced? Can we protect ourselves from accidents which might rupture the links between question and answer and abort the beauty waiting to be born in 'the deeper import of these weighty and pregnant utterances'?

One woman who made such a map was Laura Clifford Barney. She had certain qualities in common with her quiet sister, the Nightingale of Paradise, for she placed her devotion to the Covenant above all else and she worked silently in comparison with the more vociferous of her generation. Since she was a Westerner, however, she has the dubious advantage of being easier to excavate. Her family, her background, the context in which she grew up and from which she turned in recognition of the Bahá'í Cause are well known and more easily reconstructed. But she can just as easily suffer from the same erasure.

We should begin the story with Laura's mother, Alice Pike, who at the age of seventeen was taken on the European tour and introduced, while in Paris, to the explorer Henry Stanley. To say he was smitten is an understatement. He attended upon her in Paris, pursued her to London, and shortly after she returned to New York he appeared on the scene again, ostensibly to solicit funds for his return to Africa, for he was determined to cross the continent to discover the source of the River Congo. Before leaving on this historic exploration, Henry Stanley prevailed upon the seventeen-year-old girl to sign with him a marriage contract, stating that she would wait to marry him on his return, even as he pledged to marry her in that event. His commitment might be measured by the fact that he named his ship *The Lady*

Alice after her and with her in mind named, too, the rapids near Stanleypool. Her awareness of the significance of that commitment must be assessed by the announcement that appeared, barely six months later, that she was to marry Albert Barney of Dayton, Ohio, the heir to a wealthy estate.

The marriage proved tedious and Alice was openly relieved when it was over. Her husband had disapproved of her interest in art and, in complete contrast with that rather insistent young Englishman who was to bring such lustre to his name, had clearly not been much of an explorer in any particular field. She must have wondered often, in the light of subsequent events, what her fate might have been had she married the Englishman. Years later she drew his portrait, from memory; there is a piercing demand in his eye which seems to threaten the illusion any woman might have had of her independent will. It is doubtful whether his ego would have allowed hers free reign, a perception acknowledged years later when Laura asked her mother for advice about a male travelling companion for her trip to Paris. The choice was between Mason Remey and Hippolyte Dreyfus, both of whom were being sent by 'Abdu'l-Bahá to Persia, and either one, He said, 'You can choose'. Alice, remembering, perhaps, her own choices, encouraged Laura to travel in the company of the young Frenchman, Hippolyte Dreyfus because 'the other will always be thinking of himself'.[7] Some explorers are only intent upon their own discoveries. Certainly the great explorer Stanley was driven to map out and claim territories in a manner that might have both attracted and repelled the young artistic Alice. Perhaps she wished *not* to be his personal continent to explore.

Finally, at her husband's death, she was able to complete the Barney Studio in 1902, and it was from here that she conducted her own form of exploration. All kinds of artistic and esoteric events took place in this house: seances, poetry readings, '*tableaux vivants*' and musical evenings in which the aristocracy of political society participated. Plays too were performed, among which may have been one privately printed and exquisitely bound, written in 1910 by her daughter Laura, entitled *God's Heroes*, a rather stilted play about Qurratu'l-'Ayn. In this house the *literati* of Washington gathered and here, as dramas were performed and portraits painted, the boundaries of art and reality were being explored. Across the gallery where musicians sometimes played above her studio Alice had illumined the words: 'The Problem of Art is to Cause by Appearance the Illusion of a Higher Reality'. Among the portraits were several of her daughters, depicted in the 'higher realities' they had assumed in some of these dramas. Natalie, the rebel, the writer, the eldest darling who was to become a notorious lesbian with her own *salon* in Paris, stares insolently out of the canvas under the smouldering guise of Lucifer; Laura, the little one, the solemn dark-haired girl who was to espouse the Faith of Bahá'u'lláh, represent the International Council of Women in the League of Nations and become an ardent worker in the cause of world peace, glares stonily through a whirl of snakes as Medusa. In the panelled dining room where an obscene little devil ejects water into a pool of tiles, a life-size painting of a woman dressed in flowing robes now hangs. She has stepped straight out of the Book of Revelation and, crowned with twelve stars, stands upon the moon and holds the sun in her arms as a cluster of evil red-eyed snakes hover above her and are held at bay. Clearly, Alice Pike Barney and her daughters were exploring frontiers of the unknown.

But Alice Pike was an artist and not a map-maker; she did not concern herself with charting out the territories she explored. She was also a philanthropist and her sense of social conscience motivated her to bring art to the attention of the public, but there again she was perhaps too much of a bohemian ever to be a part of the stuffy Washington society she wished to cultivate.

Besides, art was part of a continent that many had explored before her, leaving their brave flags, though few had come home as successful colonizers. Whose empire could encompass the mysterious country where art ends and reality begins? Whose maps might be trusted to show at what point imagination might lose itself in swamps of delusion? What instruments could distinguish between the freedom of the soul and the drive of the insistent self? Where would one turn to discover the source of creative thinking without losing oneself in a wilderness of idle fancy? These may have been some of the matters explored through recitation and seance at the Barney Studio but if Alice raised the questions, she found no answers. It was her younger daughter Laura who was to become the meticulous map-maker, the one who was driven with the zeal of the explorer her mother did not marry, to chart out the unknown territories of the soul.

Perhaps when a child is raised in an atmosphere of questions she might either become enamoured of them for their own sake or seek with heightened zeal for answers. Natalie seemed to have made the former choice and Laura the latter. Certainly her lifelong concern with issues of justice and international peace, her careful documentation of Bahá'í teachings and her devotion to 'Abdu'l-Bahá, might seem incongruous unless it is set within the context of her upbringing.

It would have been very easy for Laura to have been erased by the flamboyance of her mother and the increasing notoriety of her sister. Certainly one would imagine in the present climate of biography-writing that researchers would first turn to those two more colourful women than to Laura, who has been indicted by the snide comment of her lifelong adviser in financial affairs as being rather a 'solemn person'. Whether this necessarily means she smiled less or was more serious-minded, the effect of the remark, as well as that imputed to her sister, is to erase her, in effect. Natalie, whose character and interests contrasted with Laura's in every way, is said to have complained that it was all very well for Laura to be doing 'good works' but did she really have to do them twenty-four hours a day?

Alice Pike had searched for truth through the arts. Her daughter Natalie continued the quest by testing the limits of socially acceptable behaviour. The manner in which Laura sought after truth was more practical and less predictable than either of these, took far more courage, and was of an infinite loneliness. She established children's hospitals and worked with war refugees; she was the only woman recognized by the League of Nations for her work in education and intellectual cooperation; she was among the first women to recognize the vital role of the media in promoting peace rather than war, and was finally honoured by the French government when she was elevated to the rank of Officier de la Legion d'Honneur. And the motivation behind all these efforts was undoubtedly her recognition and acceptance of the Bahá'í Faith.

She heard of the Faith through May Ellis Bolles in Paris at the turn of the century and shortly thereafter made her way to 'Akká and to the presence of 'Abdu'l-Bahá. Once she had met Him she wanted to absorb all He had to say. She came three times to the Holy Land between 1904 and 1906 and returned again in 1908. It is important to remember that such repeated visits would have been rare among the pilgrims at that time. Her requests to return were granted by 'Abdu'l-Bahá; perhaps she was even encouraged to return, if not actually invited to stay, because her visits were marked by practical actions and not merely questioning words. On one occasion she was able to secure the services of an excellent English teacher for 'Abdu'l-Bahá's grandson Shoghi Effendi, a step which was to have far-reaching effects for his education and subsequent achievements; on another she became instrumental in purchasing the land, arranging for the design, with 'Abdu'l-Bahá's approval, and overseeing the construction of the historic house at No 7 Haparsim Street.

During the spring of 1905 she came briefly to Europe and convinced her mother to visit 'Akká with her. Alice Pike Barney painted the portrait of the Prisoner in 'Akká and He took the trouble of calling on her three times during His visit to Washington in 1912, even stopping by the Studio house at the risk of missing His train to say good-bye on His way to the station at His departure from that city.

Laura gathered the notes of her table talks with 'Abdu'l-Bahá over these extended visits, and with His permission and correction, published her book *Some Answered Questions* in English in 1908. Balyuzi writes of the lucidity and coherence of this book, of the genius of 'Abdu'l-Bahá that it captures, of the conversational tone of His language that arrests one's attention by its 'crystal clarity' and 'flawless' reasoning, of the fact that 'Abdu'l-Bahá seems to answer with an effortless ease 'without previous intimation of the nature and purport of the query'.[8]

But what of the nature of these queries and the mind of the inquirer? We have looked at the book for its answers but haven't realized how many of them lie in the nature of the questions asked. Laura herself states in her Preface to the first edition, 'I believe that what has been so valuable to me may be of use to others, since all men, notwithstanding their differences, are united in their search for reality.'[9] Clearly there is some value for us in trying to understand her motives.

What then were some of the problems that she may have been acutely aware of in her life? What was the context of these questions? What was the practical soil of daily choice from which they arose?

Certainly there were problems of religion and of course endless problems of ethics. Alice Pike's father was a Jew who came to Cincinnati in the last century to make his fortune. He did this by first establishing a whiskey distillery and then marrying the Christian daughter of the town mayor after the latter's death. At the time it would have been unforgivable for a society girl of such standing to marry a Jew and it is easy to wonder whether all his philanthropy towards the arts in later life might have been motivated as much by a desire to find cultural acceptance in his newly-adopted society as by an instinctive love for opera.

The aesthetic absolution he might have sought curiously prefigures the wider resolutions achieved by a later generation. When his granddaughter Laura married Hippolyte Dreyfus years later, this young intellectual had already studied and accepted the Bahá'í Faith. He had been told by 'Abdu'l-Bahá that while the notorious Dreyfus, whose 'affaire' had the whole of Paris in a turmoil, had become 'famous in the world of politics . . . I pray that you will, in the Cause of God, become even more famous than he'. How Laura must have rejoiced in the way that 'Abdu'l-Bahá widened the context and resolved all conflicts of ideology in one's life! 'He spoke simply,' she writes of the Master, 'and His sentences became a part of one's inner thoughts seeking a worthy outlet in action.'[10] What, did she imagine, would have been the response of her grandfather's soul, untrammelled now by either Jewishness or whiskey, to her choice of becoming a Bahá'í? How, if not as a Bahá'í, could she have reconciled the conflicts inherent in her own background? How else but from this detached perspective could she have asked questions such as those about the resurrection and the virgin birth, about the nature of heaven and hell and the Second Coming?

Then there were related problems of truth and art. If the problem of art, as the motto of the Studio balcony announced, was to cause by appearance the illusion of a higher reality, how does one distinguish between them? Can the spiritual powers symbolized by appearances in this contingent world also be subverted? Can their persuasive messages convey evil as well as good? Is the higher reality sought for through art merely an anarchic principle or is it in turn subject to some greater governing power?

She had questions too about the relationship of the

soul and the body. She herself had a body that she was
not eager to advertise and wore long black dresses to the
end of her life which hid her little frame and conspicuous
limp; her sister, on the other hand, rather worshipped
her body, posing for early photographers in the nude.
Was it any wonder that Laura questioned 'Abdu'l-Bahá
on the nature of the soul, on the possibility of reincarna-
tion, on the distinction between the physical and the
intellectual powers? Laura's face looks down at us as a
little girl, capped like a cavalier, her body hidden; her
sister Natalie poses with a careless, narcissistic grace as
the Happy Prince, her lovely limbs lapped in green
doublet and hose. What do these different portraits tell
us of the temperamental as well as physical contrasts
between the two sisters? Does the truth lie in their outer
forms or in some hidden reality? One of Laura's questions is about 'The Causes of the Differences in the
Characters of Men'.

One senses that many of Laura's questions might have
been voiced on behalf of her mother too. Was art to be a
substitute for religion? Could the Holy Spirit descend on
the painter at her easel? What was the difference between
the knowledge possessed by man and that possessed by
the divine manifestations? What of the seances at 2306
Sheridan Circle, the 'visions and communications with
spirits'? What of spiritual healers, astrology and panthe-
ism? Since her mother believed in art as a veil through
which reality might shine, according to the philosophy of
the French symbolists, is everyone's reality the same in
spite of their differing illusions? Can there be some way
of perceiving reality so that we sense our united search
rather than our differences? Certainly Laura would have
had many questions to ask 'Abdu'l-Bahá.

Perhaps her questions were also a reflection of comparison between her marriage and her mother's. Lost among the framed heads of George Bernard Shaw and G.K. Chesterton in the Barney Studio house is the rather dim and unremarkable face of Albert Barney, deceased. Was he disapproving of her mother after his death as he had been during his life? Was he subject to the mercy of God even if he had not been altogether just towards her? Her own husband, like the husband of the silent Maryam Khánum, played a remarkable role by enabling her to be herself. Revered in Europe as the first French Bahá'í, loved dearly by 'Abdu'l-Bahá and devoted to Shoghi Effendi who depended upon him with utter trust, Hippolyte Dreyfus was Laura's companion and partner as well as her husband. He provided her with support in her travels to Persia and worked on the French translation of *Some Answered Questions* before their marriage. His preface to his own book *Essai sur le Baha'ism* is nothing but praise of Laura's work, and curiously, the qualities for which he is remembered by Shoghi Effendi all echo Laura's: his systematic meticulousness, his modesty and consideration, his hard-working efficiency. At a time when such a choice would have been revolutionary, he took her name and she kept hers when they married in 1911. Without him how could Laura have been able to pursue the goal of making sure 'that world affairs are home affairs'?[11]

Some Answered Questions is not only a gift of 'Abdu'l-Bahá's 'tired moments' to the Bahá'ís of the world; it is a testament of Laura's tireless longing for answers. Impressionable and susceptible both to the artistic ideals of her mother and the censorious practicality of her father, she must have wondered deeply and seriously about the

nature of good and evil, the distinction between prophetic
and poetic utterance, the enigma of freewill and the lure
of spiritual liberty. While her older sister rejected men,
defiantly, in her exaltation of her own sex, Laura found
as her companion in this world a man among men who
erased his own considerable achievements as a scholar
and traveller in order to assist hers. While Natalie chose
the volatility of words to express overt rebellion and
dramatized the '*tableau vivant*' of her personality in all its
beauty and egoism, Laura worked more ponderously in
stone, watched more patiently through history and,
above all, questioned.

She not only questioned the stuffy religious conventions
and hypocritical ethics of the society into which she had
been born but the bohemian fantasy-world of esoteric
and occult extravagances of her up-bringing as well. Her
husband, before he became a Bahá'í, had been an
agnostic and a sceptic, according to May Ellis Bolles,
'had never believed in any force transcending nature nor
had he received intimations of the possible existence of a
Supreme Being'.[12] His very existence was a question,
much like her own father's, of the kinds of values enacted
at 2306 Sheridan Circle. When she saw the effect of
'Abdu'l-Bahá on him, when she realized that within the
circle of 'Abdu'l-Bahá's Covenant the extremes might
meet, her instincts must have made her yearn to offer
others such resolutions. But her medium was not language with its facile assumptions, nor drama with its
public self-consciousness, nor even the showy silence of
paint, but the concealment of stone. Like the sculptress
she had been as a girl, like the builder of houses she
became as a woman, she began to chisel towards the
truth. Slowly, systematically, she began to chip away

with her questions, yearning to hold a reality in her hands that could house us all in meaning.

Her systematic nature is not only reflected in the painstaking catalogue of questions she asked but also in a brief anecdote recorded by Balyuzi, taken from the memoirs of Dr Yúnis Khán Afrúkhtih. Seated at the table in the house of 'Abdu'lláh Páshá, Miss Barney had begun questioning 'Abdu'l-Bahá on the theme of 'Evil'. 'Abdu'l-Bahá had announced that 'There is no evil in existence'. Then, 'He turned to Yúnis Khán who was acting as His interpreter and said with a smile: "Next she will ask, how is it then that God has created the scorpion." In a moment Laura Barney posed this very question. The Master remarked: "Did I not say so?" and proceeded to explain that the venom of the scorpion's sting is its means of defence, and does not constitute evil in its own milieu.'[13]

In *Some Answered Questions* 'Abdu'l-Bahá's answer is expressed in a simplicity of language that reflects Laura's own slight knowledge of Persian rather than, as she notes in the Preface, the 'extensive command of felicitous expressions'[14] instinctive to 'Abdu'l-Bahá: '. . . it is possible that one thing in relation to another may be evil, and at the same time within the limits of its proper being it may not be evil.'[15] It would be so easy to mistake such simplicity for pedantry. It would be equally facile to assume her care and precision were due to a lack of imagination, a dullness of vision. One gasps with surprise at the recollection that the woman who meticulously set down the account of these questions and answers in her interviews with a little-known Prisoner in the fortress city of 'Akká was to be showered with honours and public acknowledgements by the French government at her death several decades later. For she was not only a Bahá'í in name but in deed too. She not only mapped out an interior journey through the new world of ethical values and spiritual perceptions but proceeded to explore it, step by practical step, through her social and educational work for the League of Nations.

Her humility, however, makes her keenly aware of her limitations. In her Preface, she apologizes beforehand for the simplicity of her map: 'In my case', she writes, 'the teachings were made simple, to correspond to my rudimentary knowledge . . .'[16] Perhaps the only way to evaluate that humility is to see it in the context provided by her husband, whose equally modest words highlight her remarkable achievement: 'By this work', he writes of *Some Answered Questions*,

> Laura Clifford Barney has powerfully contributed to placing within the reach of the public the teachings of the new religion . . . *Some Answered Questions*, therefore, covers a deficiency particularly perceptible in the West . . . The great spread of Bahaism in England and America has prompted me to publish also in English this essay that I have just brought out in France and which I offer to the intelligent interlocutor of *Some Answered Questions* as a modest addition to her work.

8

And the Law

We are accustomed to maps of the body: X-rays, cardiographs, a multitude of tests that screen our blood, our bones, our very breath. The extraordinary advances in science have made such maps increasingly more subtle and revealed in the process that our knowledge is disconcertingly less precise than we would have liked to imagine. Confronted by these uncertainties we have recently been attempting to explore the regions of strangeness, turbulence and random behaviour and have admitted the inadequacy of our earlier over-simplified maps by looking into chaos for principles of order that Newton and Euclid simply overlooked. Finally, because of the sheer multiplicity of experts, we are gradually becoming weaned from the opinions of the few. We are learning, slowly, not to make priests of our scientists and to keep the mind open to alternative interpretations.

We are less accustomed to maps of the soul, however, and more tolerant of inaccuracies in these. Spiritual codes have always proliferated, easily been broken, and are continually being reconstructed from the left-over fragments. But strangely enough, although our knowledge in this area is notoriously imprecise, we have a curious tendency towards over-simplification and absolutism when it comes to charting spiritual matters. The salvation of the soul has repeatedly depended on rigid

formulas of behaviour. Philosophies, each bolstered by
rigorous argument, have ranged from extreme pessimism
to blind utopian optimism. Through the advances in
science, however, we are beginning to realize that the
relativity of truth is not a principle to be applied to
physical matters alone. Mystics and poets and martyrs
have often been more fervently convinced by their own
codes than successful in convincing anyone else. We may
soon acknowledge that uncertainty, with its implication
of trust, is a spiritual condition as vital to our inner
development as it is to quantum mechanics.

In both scientific and religious matters clearly more is
needed than the code. The laws of the physical and
spiritual universe both depend on some other element –
call it intuition or faith, call it Imagination, as Blake did
– which carries the mind into uncharted territories and
sustains it in that journey, in order to travel on a beam of
light or conceive of a world at peace; some other element
that enters the comprehension and educates the habits of
the whole crowd and not just a few individuals in it;
something that penetrates the heart and moves secretly
and silently through the blood of the multitude; something that infuses an entire society with new vigour,
transforms a civilization with fresh impulses. Wine is
needed.

> Think not that We have revealed unto you a mere code
> of laws. Nay, rather, We have unsealed the choice
> Wine with the fingers of might and power . . . Meditate
> upon this, O men of insight![1]

Before getting to the wine and its distinction from the
mere code of laws, which is the subject of meditation in
this last essay, I would like to glance briefly at two

interesting ideas in the Bahá'í teachings that seem connected with the idea of maps and their limitations. One is that everyone should write a will. The other is that graveyards should be places where we might wish to walk and think and meditate. Bahá'u'lláh encourages us, when in distress, to visit graveyards in order that we might consider the evanescence of this temporal world. And 'Abdu'l-Bahá even goes so far as to design a cemetery, with paths running parallel and many trees, encircling a fountain.[2] The map He offers is far from an ideal we must slavishly follow: it is rather a reminder of a far more complex and individualized map which one must chart for oneself. I would venture to suggest that the essentials of this map have nothing to do with the position of paths or fountains. The plan of the cemetery, in other words, is not a substitute for its purpose. This could be reflected in a multitude of other designs, so long as the salient features in 'Abdu'l-Bahá's example are maintained and observed.

Instead of relating the 'salient features' solely to construction plans, I wonder whether they might not be connected with something less tangible, to whatever would make the place conducive to an upliftment of the heart, an opening of the faculties, a detachment of the spirit. The graveyard should not be a place either of gloom or of dread; its atmosphere is not intended to provoke fear or even anxiety, in the old traditional sense of horror of the unknown. Instead this place compels thoughtfulness, quietude. It encourages a deepening of one's appreciation for the precious opportunities that life offers. It awakens an awareness that life is transitory even as it is so precious. It is like a retreat. One who walks along these paths and past these fountains, one who reads the silent headstones and prays for the tranquil dead, one who considers the turbulence of these spent lives and listens to the bird song overhead and sees the trees stand patiently and feels the evening breeze against his cheek will surely think, 'Seize thy chance, for it will come to thee no more!'[3] And simultaneously he will think, 'Abandon not the everlasting beauty for a beauty that must die, and set not your affections on this mortal world of dust.'[4]

The graveyard is an abstract map of life. When we actually step on these paths and enter the reality of this map, we experience the paradox of living: we are pulled by the desire to participate fully in the everyday wonders around us and simultaneously we are drawn back, like spectators, so that we see it fleeting by. It is an experience, in short, very like that felt by the audience at a play. It is, moreover, at its highest expression, the experience of being an angel of fire and snow, protected from both extremities, discovering truth to be the interaction between them.

The injunction to write a will and testament seems to have a similar aim. It is intended that by taking stock of our lives and considering our priorities, by evaluating our material belongings and articulating our spiritual goals we might keep ourselves aligned, as it were. We might thereby remind ourselves that a day will surely come when this particular configuration of atoms we call our person will have vanished into thin air and all that will remain of us is what we may have done, how we may have affected the lives of others. How urgent, therefore, the need to be attuned, now, at this very moment, so that our actions will be conducive to the well-being and harmony of the human race. Our beliefs are what we evaluate in writing our will and not merely our effects.

Most importantly, however, is our recognition that these beliefs are the salient reasons for our writing a will. It is not intended to be a mere code. Like the 'wine' in the well-known quotation from the *Aqdas*, it suggests a far more subtle, invisible, incalculable process that is taking place within. The content of the will, therefore, and its relation to our personal effects, is to be clearly distinguished from the testament. The significance of this elusive distinction between the code and the wine reminds us of the lesson learned by 'Abdu'l-Karím about the meaning of true scholarship. If we embark upon the dubious task of questioning the significance and application of religious law we revert to that whole tradition of religious jurisprudence that gave rise to some of the most narrow-minded fundamentalists in the past. We need to remember the process of detachment undergone by the true scholar as we pursue these questions. Like 'Abdu'l-Karím we need first to discover the belief beneath the behest of Bahá'u'lláh about the laws of inheritance.

It seems to me that a great deal is at stake when we approach Bahá'í laws. These too provide a kind of map; they offer clues about the continuously shifting terrain of interaction between the individual and society. It is a mistake to imagine they are closed, self-contained and absolute systems of thought. Like the concept of 'phase space' in modern physics, they show a single point only in a single instant of time, for what they signify is a dynamic system, a continuously changing and moving and fluctuating condition. Bahá'u'lláh's laws, like a 'flexible road map to all possibilities', need to be set in their dynamic context and can only be grasped in their fullness when we actually undertake the journey into the wilderness, step by step, when we understand what beliefs are implicit in the laws – rather than measure by the laws the dimensions of belief – when we taste the wine they contain.

In the spirit of those early scholars, therefore, and those heroes who found freedom in obedience to God, let us question, with as much spiritual maturity as we can pretend to, the nature of Bahá'í law. The first impression one has of this religion is that it has so few laws. The laws of prohibition against the taking of drugs and alcohol, the laws with regard to parental consent for marriage and most recently the laws of the Ḥuqúqu'lláh are the only ones in the category of social laws that we have been asked to consider, and not even all of those are binding everywhere. The other laws of a more spiritual nature, related to fasting, obligatory prayers and burial rites, belong in the personal category and cannot really be defined as social laws in the same sense. Most curious of all is the fact that although we have a book of laws, the *Kitáb-i-Aqdas*, this book is far less familiar to us than a book of prayers and meditations, a book of Tablets written to the kings and rulers of the earth, a book of proofs. Indeed, it is only now undergoing translation and is known to the majority of Bahá'ís in the form of the *Synopsis and Codification of the Kitáb-i-Aqdas* collated by Shoghi Effendi and completed for publication by the Universal House of Justice in 1973. This *Synopsis*, moreover, far from elucidating the significance of Bahá'í law, has provoked more questions about it. Only by the end of this present Plan, in 1992, is it envisioned that we will actually be able to read for ourselves Bahá'u'lláh's *Most Holy Book* and the *Questions and Answers* addendum which is a part of it. Certainly it would seem there are many

areas of ignorance we must immediately acknowledge
when it comes to the subject of Bahá'í law.

Maybe the best way to define our own ignorance is by
looking at characteristics which seem common to the
laws of this Revelation. The initial characteristic that
seems noteworthy about Bahá'u'lláh's laws is the language
in which He chooses to refer to them. He calls them
'sweet-smelling'; He suggests they are like wine, like suns
that illumine the horizons of our minds. One thing they
are not: images of constraint in either case.

A secondary characteristic of Bahá'í law to which the
language itself gives rise is that it is frequently symbolic.
A law gives physical shape to an inward and spiritual
condition. The recital of prayers, for instance, according to a letter of Shoghi Effendi dated 5 November
1934 quoted in a recent memorandum from the Research
Department of the Universal House of Justice, is a 're-
gulation(s)' whose significance is 'thus purely spiritual'.[5]
The giving of a dowry, too, is a 'symbolic act'.[6]

Another aspect of Bahá'í law linked to its symbolic
nature finds expression in the metaphor of the seed. The
metaphor which recalls both the wine and the sun from
Bahá'u'lláh's own language carries connotations of the
passage of time, the period of gestation required, the
significance of the process of comprehension as against
static or theoretical knowledge. The *Kitáb-i-Aqdas*, writes
the House of Justice in a letter to the National Spiritual
Assembly of Iceland dated 23 January 1976, is similar to
a 'kernel' whose import needs time and gestation in the
soil of human evolution to bear its fruitful meaning.[7]

A final characteristic of the laws of Bahá'u'lláh seems
to be that they are in some cases a means to fill the voids
that we ourselves create. In the case of intestacy, for

instance, or 'in the absence of . . . specific arrangements' in the case of divorce,[8] we find there is a law which can apply. Law in such instances is a substitute for chaos rather than for personal choice. Perhaps even, with modern physics in mind, it is a glimmer of the order underlying chaos. It comes into force when we ourselves have not assumed personal responsibility for our lives.

In these brief inconclusive assumptions about Bahá'í law, three significant principles seem to emerge, principles which Shoghi Effendi enumerates as being characteristic of 'the Faith standing identified with the name of Bahá'u'lláh'.[9] They are the relativity, the continuity and the progressive nature of truth. In addition to these cardinal principles, moreover, are a host of others which in a sense are the methods of application we have grown accustomed to recognize as distinctively *Bahá'í* in nature: the principle of sexual equality, of the significance of diversity, of the importance of the consultative process, of the independent investigation of truth, and of the correspondence between scientific knowledge and religious belief, to name the most obvious. All these, grounded in the belief that truth must be relative, must express a continuity of thought and action and must necessarily be progressive in its nature, would seem to be ground rules by which means our ignorance can measure the meaning of Bahá'u'lláh's laws.

Of all these distinctive Bahá'í principles, the one which I find most challenging in the context of the laws of the *Kitáb-i-Aqdas* relates to the principle of the equality of men and women. Evoking the spirit of true scholarship embodied in 'Abdu'l-Karím and Vahíd, therefore, and the courage of Ṭáhirih to challenge priestcraft and fundamentalism, I would like to ask some questions

about Bahá'í laws in the light of this principle. Since
women have traditionally been linked to death, and it is
that particular tradition that Bahá'u'lláh has reversed,
we might as well start where we ended, with the will.

In the *Synopsis and Codification of the Kitáb-i-Aqdas*
under 'Laws, Ordinances and Exhortations' we find
among others related to personal status the laws which
Bahá'u'lláh revealed for inheritance, that is, the law with
regard to how an individual's estate should be divided in
cases of intestacy. In both the last item relating to
inheritance and note 25, which provides further elucida-
tion by Shoghi Effendi, it is stressed that this code
applies 'only to such cases when a Bahá'í dies without
leaving a will and when, therefore, his property will have
to be divided in accordance with the rules set forth in the
Aqdas'.[10] From the outset we have to realize that a map is
being provided for those who have not attempted the
journey for themselves. It can be, if we choose, a prototype, but Shoghi Effendi does not anywhere indicate
that this is the case. It would be up to an individual to
make it so. Like the plan for the ideal graveyard, it can
also be changed so long as the essential features which it
contains are grasped and applied. As has been stressed
already, we have to know what those essential features of
belief are in order to understand how they sustain the
structure of a law.

The first thing we notice is that the children take
precedence over the husband or wife of the deceased.
Why should this be so? What does it imply about the
rights and responsibilities of children and parents? Does
it imply that children have priority for financial independence over the continuing independence of the parent?
Does it rather suggest that they have a prior responsibility

at the death of one parent for the well-being of the other?
The Bahá'í principle of relationships between family
members is implicit here, the definition of an equality
based on everyone's rights and responsibilities towards
everyone else. It is interesting to note that at this juncture, moreover, no distinction is made between the man
or the woman as a surviving parent. In other words, if a
woman dies, her husband has no more right over the properties of his dead wife than if the widow had been left.
In the past when children inherited at the death of the
father, widows were often very vulnerable. They were
either abandoned to destitution where remarriage was
frowned upon or forced into remarriage in order to relieve
the children of being financially responsible for them. In
some cases they lost all rights of access to their children,
in others they had to relinquish whatever remained of
their original dowry settlement. Only for a certain period
and in very specialized areas of Europe during the four-
teenth century was widowhood actually extolled as an
enviable and independent state, and then only in relation
to the other alternatives open to women. Never before
have widowers been granted the same station of vulnerability.

So far so good. None of these ideas seems in any way
contradictory to the essential characteristic of equality in
the Faith. If we cannot all have the same rights then at
least let us have equal loss of rights. But when we reach
the third, fourth, fifth and sixth categories of the will we
begin to get into trouble if we have been looking at the
laws for clues about principles, rather than bringing the
established principles to shed light upon the laws.

Why in each case should the father and the brother get
priority before the mother and the sister? Why are the

women being penalized? Why in this hierarchy does it seem that the principle of sexual equality is being violated? More outrageous seems the discrimination amongst the offspring which provides that while the boys receive the principal residence, the girls get no more than the mother's used clothing. Worst of all, it appears that if there are full brothers and sisters, those from the mother's side do not inherit at all.

With these questions unresolved it is impossible to look at any other of Bahá'u'lláh's laws and not find more examples of what we have assumed to be 'inequality'. Why, for instance, are there apparent discriminations in provisions conditioned on the virginity of the wife? Why should 'women in their courses' be granted exemptions in performance of obligatory prayers and ablutions, especially since the exemptions do not provide for a shorter length of time spent on the prayer? Whereas such exemptions might make sense if they were provided for the ease of physical discomfort, why does it appear from the length of time still required that the difference in wording simply emphasizes connotations of ritual impurity in past religious and cultural practices? Why on earth should Bahá'u'lláh validate the dowry system when clearly the exchange of gifts on the occasion of marriage carries centuries of evil connotations for women? How can any of these laws coincide with the principle of the equality of men and women?

In the back of our minds we hear echoes of those two sisters threatening to storm out of the house with nothing but their veils. Would their reactions have been so inclined to offended pride, would they have triggered the suspicions of their brother if the laws of inheritance had not awarded him twice as much as it awarded them?

Indeed, how have women traditionally fared under the law, religious or secular? Has it not always inclined them towards subversion, since it has so rarely protected their interests? Is it not our instinct, as it was those sisters', to distrust the efficacy of any law and take affairs into our own hands, to the degree that we can? In other words, even as our hackles are raised and we question these laws, we need to bear in mind our own female tradition in response to any law, which is subversion, concealed rebellion: the habits of adolescence.

We have never had the luxury of living in a society based on principles of equality between the sexes. We therefore assume, as do those who say there will never be peace because there has always been war, that any law we read about is grounded in a psychology of inequality. This is perfectly understandable. What we are reacting to are not the laws themselves but the connotations that have accrued over the centuries to certain associations which we find in the laws. I would like to look at these associations more closely and question our reactions to them as women and as anyone who assumes he or she believes in sexual equality.

The first association I would like to question relates to symbology. Why, oh why are women always linked by symbol to biology and men always linked to economics? The most dramatic example of this association in Bahá'u-'lláh's *Aqdas* occurs with reference to the dowry. It might be useful to look for a moment at some of the unpleasant connotations here and then question Bahá'u'lláh's application of them.

The exchange of money between people has always been associated with the sale of property. When it is linked to marriage it reverberates with centuries of sexual abuse. It is hard for women, whose bodies have in so many cultures been assessed as male property and who have, even in recent history, been perceived as no more than domestic slaves, to understand this act as 'symbolic' without assuming the worst about the symbolism. Certainly we cannot claim to come to this law with uncluttered minds. Can men? When a man gives a woman money to 'seal' a marriage bond can he do so without unconsciously dramatizing his 'ownership' of her? The archetypal imagery here is very powerful. Its associations and connotations are undeniably strong. Bahá'u'lláh chooses no limp and pallid symbol in which to couch His law. He chooses one that has the accumulated weight of centuries of significance.

We can either assume that Bahá'u'lláh did not really understand the full significance of His own enunciated principle of equality or that He intended this law to reflect it. We can either conclude that He did not have the vision to know where it might lead in the future when He gave us a law that was clearly rooted in the past, or we can pause a moment and wonder whether it is rather our own reactions that are so rooted and bound by tradition. Has it not been the distinguishing characteristic of the Manifestations of God that they take the symbolic gestures of an old and decaying civilization and transform them, revolutionize them, reverse their meaning? What would be the point of reversing the meaning of human actions that are not particularly charged with emotional weight, that are innocuous enough whichever way they stand?

Something like this reversal surely happened in the paradigmatic shift between the meaning of sacrifice in Judaism as symbolized in the story of Abraham and

Isaac and the far more reverberative meaning which
sacrifice assumed in the context of Christ's martyrdom
on the cross. In both episodes we have common elements:
father/son relations; the test of obedience; the spilling of
blood, threatened in one story and enacted in the other;
the theme of grace, redemption and forgiveness. The
difference between the stories, however, is what makes
them remarkable, and the most significant difference is
one of scale. This can be sensed in the difference between
being offered as a sacrifice by another and offering
oneself, which depend on different degrees of awareness.
It can also be measured in the movement from willing
intent to completed action. The main point is that we
would not be able to appreciate the sense of relativity,
continuity or progression of these religious truths had the
symbol not already been charged with old meanings and
familiar at a different scale of significance, had it not
been deeply ingrained and heavily weighted with emotion.

To compare great things with small, therefore, perhaps the same may be true of the transformation implicit
in this one little law related to the giving and receiving of
a dowry. In order to understand the nature of these
transformations maybe we could return to that assumption I first expressed: that men have been and are always
associated with money and women with bodies, that
men's 'world' had been defined by economics and
women's by biology. Certainly it would seem at first
glance that this generalization seems to be re-echoed in
Bahá'í law. Men are supposed to be primarily responsible
for the upkeep of the family which suggests they do the
majority of earning during a woman's childbearing
years. Men have to provide for the livelihood of the wife
during the year of patience. They have the prime

responsibility for the schooling of the children. In the light of these economic duties it is the son who is the primary inheritor of the will for in this religion as in so many others the law of primogeniture is in effect. It is the man, as we have noted, who must pay the 'symbolic' dowry to the wife. Clearly the man and his money are closely linked.

But what is significant here, as in the case of sacrifice, are the differences in the implications of these laws. Set against the connotations of the past where the man/money equation spelt a single word – power – we find, on the contrary that every reference to a man having money, in the context of Bahá'u'lláh's laws, relates to his loss of power. He is associated with money but none of it belongs to him. The reason he inherits it, according to a letter written by the Universal House of Justice to a National Assembly on 28 December 1980, is because he has 'the responsibility to care for his mother', to say nothing of the primary responsibility he has to support any wife or children he might have of his own. So little power does he have over money that a husband has no explicit right, as does the wife, of being supported by his spouse. The reason he is considered the 'head' of the household is because he must assume the burden of educating all the children in it.[11] The symbolic act of the dowry-giving, then, takes on a whole different meaning. When a man marries he is giving up the traditional power associated with money. Instead of an act that implies ownership, it has become a gesture that symbolizes relinquishment of that old patriarchal concept.

This reversal has to be set against many other ideas and ordinances in the Faith. For the old connotations of dowry-giving to remain true the woman must still be dependent on the man for her financial means. If we look closely at Bahá'u'lláh's teachings we see that this cannot possibly be the case. To begin with, from childhood the girl has priority in all educational benefits. She has to be trained in all the sciences and arts in equal measure and to the same standards as any boy. She must be given the qualifications, in other words, for holding her own in the fields of law and agriculture, the humanities and the sciences. She should clearly be just as capable of working and earning her livelihood as a man. When Bahá'u'lláh cautions against 'those idle and worthless souls',[12] when He clearly exhorts 'every one to engage in crafts and professions',[13] when He encourages us to 'earn a livelihood by [our] calling'[14] He is not speaking to half the human race. Women must surely be included. They, like men, have the privilege and duty as Bahá'ís to give personally to the fund. They, like men, have a spiritual obligation to pay their ḥuqúqu'lláh. They can do none of these things if they are continually and forever dependent on their fathers and their brothers, their husbands and their sons for money. They have been educated so that they can fulfil these very obligations. They do not need a man's symbolic gift, on the occasion of marriage, to make them feel they are at last being given a degree of financial independence they never had before. Certainly, as educated women of independent means, as women moreover who have learned to see themselves as created noble, as spiritual beings, they would hardly be willing to sell their bodies so cheap either, symbolically or not. The dowry must obviously mean something different to women than it used to do.

Let us consider for a moment the other side of the equation: that women are always bound by references to their bodies and connected by association to biology and no more. Certainly, as we noted already, it would appear at first glance that Bahá'u'lláh is strapping women to the same old wheel with His references to 'courses' and virginity. In relation to this last point, however, we need to recall, from the letters of the Universal House of Justice, one written to an individual in February 1982 which clarifies once and for all that 'where Bahá'u'lláh has expressed a law as between a man and a woman it applies, *mutatis mutandis*, between a woman and a man unless the context should make this impossible'.[15]

The relationship between the sexes on the subject of virginity is surely an example of this principle. Chastity in the Bahá'í writings is not a female dilemma; it is a challenge and exhortation applied to both sexes equally. Indeed, if pressure might be made to bear on either sex more than the other it would seem that Bahá'u'lláh has tipped the scales in order to admonish men more strongly than women in this matter. Writing of the criteria of a true believer He speaks of detachment in these significant terms:

> And if he met the fairest and most comely of women, he would not feel his heart seduced by the least shadow of desire for her beauty. Such an one, indeed, is the creation of spotless chastity.[16]

The test of detachment here rests precisely on the old patriarchal idea of ownership. There is nothing to suggest that a man should be impervious to beauty but that he should not wish to possess it, lay claim on it. In this admonishment we hear, for the first time in any religious tradition, words that might loosen the chains that women have had on their bodies for centuries. For the first time men must be responsible for their own desires. The woman is not the seductress. Her beauty is not to be blamed. But the man himself must guard against the seduction of the old patriarchal desire to own, to lay claim, to possess for himself, to reduce the beauty and body of a woman to the weight of a few pieces of gold.

Virginity is clearly not the only law that applies *mutatis mutandis*; the stipulations regarding travel and promises of return, separation and remarriage can all, without violating the context, apply to both men and women. In the laws applicable to marriage also it would seem obvious that a 'plurality' of husbands is just as much a violation of Bahá'í principles as a 'plurality of wives'. If one cannot marry one's step-mother then presumably one cannot marry one's step-father either. And if it is unlawful to become engaged to a girl before she reaches the age of maturity then it is equally unlawful to get engaged to a baby boy, for as Bahá'u'lláh has earlier established, 'marriage is conditioned upon both parties having attained the age of maturity'.[17] In what cases, then, does *mutatis mutandis* not apply? Where is the recipient of Bahá'u'lláh's law clearly intended to be a woman and where a man?

It is at this point that our reactions define our prejudices and we reflect the limitations of our cultural backgrounds. The fact of the matter is that the last question has brought us up against the basic physiological difference between the sexes and on this subject more than on any other we must still reckon with our instinctive reactions. Just as the dowry issue may have raised one's female hackles even as it raised male eyebrows, so too references to female biology tend to send us scurrying in different directions. Those from a traditional, particularly Islamic background will wish to keep the matter undiscussed. It will appear unseemly, vulgar and wholly out of keeping with proper 'Bahá'í' modesty to bring up such issues as menstruation for serious discussion. Those from a Western and particularly 'liberated' culture will be outraged by what appear to be 'un-Bahá'í' connotations of uncleanness and ritual impurity in these laws and exemptions. Both reactions reflect the tremendous symbolic weight that a woman's body has been made to bear in the past. Like the transaction of money and in many cases linked to it, the female body has been the unwitting container of a mass of superstition, prejudice, mangled truth and outrageous myth for centuries. It is very hard to approach the words of Bahá'u'lláh with untainted minds. Even those of us most adamant about opposing such prejudices betray the degree to which we have been affected by them through our verbal outrage, and those most earnest to avoid the subject expose the same susceptibilities by our silent prudity.

Such reactions are all understandable in the light of historical events. Women can hardly be blamed for being rather suspicious of religious laws that are ostensibly to 'protect' their rights. The meaning of law has been so perverted in the past and is so manipulated in the present that one's immediate reaction to *any* law is guarded distrust. Conditioned by past abuses and unhinged by the present litigation suits, our minds tend towards attitudes of confrontation. We feel the law is 'out to get us'; we feel it is intended as a removal of privileges, a curbing of freedoms. Women, in particular, who have been forced to assume subversive attitudes in a society in which they have been unconditionally penalized by the laws, tend to react to the law either with immense docility or with belligerent rebelliousness. We know that whenever we have been singled out in the past by religious law to be recipients of any kind of special attention, which may like the veil have originally been intended as enabling principles, these special laws have, in a male-dominated society, finally become a means of restraining the freedom, limiting the choices and crippling women from the achievement of their full potential. Thus weighed down by all this baggage from the past and all our disillusionment with the present it is hard for us to approach the question of Bahá'í laws, and in particular their application to women's bodies, without immediately taking offence.

If Bahá'u'lláh mentions women in a particular context we are offended; if He doesn't, we are offended. Whether He speaks or remains silent we react defensively. Clearly, we need not only to scrutinize His laws, therefore, but also our own reactions. And those of us who assume we understand His meaning because it confirms our own particular prejudices need to examine our complacence too. No law of God has ever confirmed humanity's complacence. Its purpose has always been to revolution-ize society and set it on a completely new basis of belief. First and foremost, therefore, we should strive to grasp His intent and not our own. Bahá'u'lláh could have given us volumes of explanation but if we have not grasped His intent we would be none the wiser.

How does one gauge intent through the medium of language? How does one drink the choice wine in His laws? How does the vehicle of expression, the container into which we pour our meanings, the cup of service in which we offer our love, the Administrative Order which carries the lifeblood of the Covenant through the limbs and members of mankind – how do these outer things remain a pure channel for the inner spirit? What lies at the heart of our Faith and provides a firm hub on which the wheel of our questions about laws relating to men and women can revolve?

At the centre of Bahá'u'lláh's wheel of unity there is the principle of equality which should govern everything we understand about His laws. The fact of the matter is that Bahá'u'lláh's intention is equality, His motivation is equality, the underlying standards of all these laws is equality. The Universal House of Justice enunciated this very simply when it wrote in a letter to an individual believer in 1974,

> The equality of men and women, as 'Abdu'l-Bahá has often explained, is a fundamental principle of Bahá'u'lláh, therefore the Laws of the Aqdas should be studied in the light of this.[18]

The next idea we need to reiterate, once we have reminded ourselves of the fundamental principle of equality, is the clear distinction made in the Writings between this and the similarity of functions. 'Equality between men and women', writes the House of Justice, 'does not, indeed physiologically it cannot, mean identity of functions'.[19] This physiological distinction is further-more qualified by 'Abdu'l-Bahá when He writes that 'Equality of men and women, *except in some negligible instances*, has been fully and categorically announced.'[20]

Then there are innumerable instances elucidated by both the Guardian and the Universal House of Justice, that these instances due to ' "physiological reasons" ...

do not reflect the inferiority or unworthiness of women'. Associated with such reasons we find Bahá'u'lláh's 'exemptions' in the *Kitáb-i-Aqdas* which, according to the Universal House of Justice should not be interpreted as 'prohibitions'. They are intended as 'an option rather than a requirement' and should 'enable, rather than prevent'.[21] All these exceptions are connected to differences of sex and age when it comes to fasting and saying of obligatory prayers, and should in no way be perceived as a distinction of ability or value between the members of the human family.

So much for the ideal wheel of intent and its various spokes. How can we ensure that we approach the laws of Bahá'u'lláh in the light of these? Unfortunately we do the reverse all the time: we approach His intention in the light of His laws. Scholarship has made it a habit in us. It is usual in the study of anthropology, history, psychology, even literary criticism to make assumptions about the principles that govern people on the basis of an interpretation of the laws they live by, the habits and customs they follow, the words they use, the gestures they employ. We have to reverse this process. We must revolutionize the way we comprehend laws, not as the clues to a belief system but as the receptacles of it. First we strengthen the belief, establish the underlying philosophy, nurture the seeds of a whole new harvest of instincts, both spiritual and social, and then we find ourselves informed of the true nature of our laws. The laws, in and of themselves, tell us nothing about spiritual principles. In fact, laws, by their very nature, can be made to follow all kinds of masters and be made to serve all kinds of contradictory principles. Our challenge is to question our assumptions, recognize the degree to which we carry around the remnants of the past, and refurbish our minds with attitudes grounded in Bahá'u'lláh's new principles before we can adequately gauge His intention. As the Universal House of Justice has cautioned already, Bahá'u'lláh's Book of Laws is:

> . . . rich in allusion and referring to laws and practices of previous Dispensations, [and] could easily be misconstrued by anyone unfamiliar with such laws and practices, insufficiently versed in the Teachings of Bahá'u'lláh and not thoroughly informed of His fundamental purposes.[22]

To ask questions about Bahá'u'lláh's purposes may not bring us any closer to an answer but it may help us pause and ponder over our own prejudices. Breaking the husk of preconceptions is necessary if the kernel of truth about these laws is to sprout; and as we have been discovering, there are a great many preconceptions we carry around about the nature of women and the ambiguity of power. There are many kernels waiting to sprout as we begin to explore the laws of Bahá'u'lláh and equality is one of them. As the Universal House of Justice, through its Research Department, wrote in a memo on this subject on 5 August 1987,

> To properly understand that Book (the *Kitáb-i-Aqdas*) one should also read many other Tablets of Bahá'u'lláh relating to them, as well as the interpretations of 'Abdu'l-Bahá and the Guardian, and realize that great areas of detail have been left by Bahá'u'lláh for the Universal House of Justice to fill in and vary in accordance with the needs of a developing society.[23]

*

It was because I had questions about the application and significance of Bahá'u'lláh's laws that I started these essays. It was because I realized that many of the world's greatest religions constructed a labyrinth of absolutes and laid the foundations of fundamentalism on the basis of jursiprudence that I sought for ways in which the Faith was different. It was, in particular, because of the traditional equation in religious history between women and the law, which has always been associated with a patriarchal social order, that I turned to Bahá'í history to seek for signs of Bahá'u'lláh's transmuting power in the affairs of the world.

His dispensation is to be known for the single and best-beloved attribute of justice. The institutions He has established are potential 'houses of justice' and at their head is the Universal House of Justice. When we consider the degree of research and study that will evolve around Bahá'u'lláh's Book of Laws we might pause for a moment in some awe and ponder the context from which we have emerged and the revolutionary concepts towards which we strive. When we think of the dangers in past religions when religious jurisprudence has overtaken the simple apprehension of truth, when we think of how scholars and priests have assumed roles of authority in the land, when we consider how easily we have been prey to fundamentalism, how questions of interpretation have been used to manipulate the masses, how women have repeatedly found themselves penalized by laws grounded in religious tradition that perceived them as male property, then maybe we can appreciate the tremendous challenge that lies before us.

The conference at Badasht occurred that we might remember it throughout this dispensation as a prototype.

The individuals immortalized in the pages of *The Dawn-Breakers* stand by us as exemplars and companions, questioning with the same earnest zeal, striving for familiar detachment from the very traditions that enabled them to recognize the truth of the Báb. The women, too, who have arisen throughout Bahá'í history with such courage both in the East and the West all await us, rank upon rank, eager to see our efforts in changing the age-long habits, assisting us with all the powers of the Concourse, applauding our endeavours to be worthy of this new, this most resplendent Cause. I wrote these essays to encourage myself to respond to them.

Bibliography

'Abdu'l-Bahá. *Memorials of the Faithful*. Translated by Marzieh Gail. Wilmette, Illinois: Bahá'í Publishing Trust, 1971.

—— *Selections from the Writings of 'Abdu'l-Bahá*. Compiled by the Research Department of the Universal House of Justice and translated by a Committee at the Bahá'í World Centre and by Marzieh Gail. Haifa: Bahá'í World Centre, 1978.

—— *Some Answered Questions*. Translated by Laura Clifford Barney. Wilmette, Illinois: Bahá'í Publishing Trust, rev. edn. 1981.

—— *A Traveller's Narrative*. Translated by Prof. Edward G. Browne. Wilmette, Illinois: Bahá'í Publishing Trust, rev. edn. 1980.

Bahá'u'lláh. *Gleanings from the Writings of Bahá'u'lláh*. Translated by Shoghi Effendi. Wilmette, Illinois: Bahá'í Publishing Trust, 1963.

—— *The Hidden Words of Bahá'u'lláh*. Translated by Shoghi Effendi. Wilmette, Illinois: Bahá'í Publishing Trust, 1982.

—— *Kitáb-i-Íqán: The Book of Certitude*. Translated by Shoghi Effendi. Wilmette, Illinois: Bahá'í Publishing Trust, 1954.

—— *The Seven Valleys and the Four Valleys*. Translated by Marzieh Gail (with Ali-Kuli Khan). Wilmette, Illinois: Bahá'í Publishing Trust, rev. edn. 1978.

—— *A Synopsis and Codification of the Kitáb-i-Aqdas*. Haifa: Bahá'í World Centre, 1973.

—— *Tablets of Bahá'u'lláh revealed after the Kitáb-i-Aqdas*. Compiled by the Research Department of the Universal House of Justice and translated by Habib Taherzadeh with the assistance of a Committee at the Bahá'í World Centre. Haifa: Bahá'í World Centre, 1978.

Balyuzi, H.M. *'Abdu'l-Bahá*. Oxford: George Ronald, 1971.

Browne, E.G. (compiler) *Materials for the Study of the Bábí Religion*. Cambridge: University Press, 1961.

Dreyfus-Barney, Laura. 'Only a Word'. *Bahá'í World*, vol. V (1932–4). New York City: Bahá'í Publishing Committee, 1936.

Hornby, Helen (compiler). *Lights of Guidance: A Bahá'í Reference File*. New Delhi, India: Bahá'í Publishing Trust, rev. edn. 1988.

Keynes, Sir Geoffrey (ed.), *Sir Thomas Browne, Selected Writings*. London: Faber, 1968.

Langer, Walter C. *The Mind of Adolf Hitler: The Secret War-Time Report*. New York: Basic Books, 1972.

Midgley, Mary, and Hughes, Judith. *Women's Choices*. London: Weidenfeld and Nicolson, 1983.

Momen, Moojan. *The Bábí and Bahá'í Religions, 1844–1944: Some Contemporary Western Accounts*. Oxford: George Ronald, 1981.

Mottahedeh, Roy. *The Mantle of the Prophet: Religion and Politics in Iran*. London: Chatto and Windus, 1985.

Nabíl-i-A'zam. *The Dawn-Breakers: Nabíl's Narrative of the Early Days of the Bahá'í Revelation*. Translated from the original Persian and edited by Shoghi Effendi. Wilmette, Illinois: Bahá'í Publishing Trust, 1962.

Rilke, Rainer Maria. *The Notebooks of Malte Laurids Brigge*. Translated by M.D. Norton. New York: Norton, 1964.

Shoghi Effendi. *Call to the Nations: Extracts from the Writings of Shoghi Effendi*. Haifa: Bahá'í World Centre, 1977.

—— *God Passes By*. Wilmette, Illinois: Bahá'í Publishing Trust, 1970.

—— *The World Order of Bahá'u'lláh*. Wilmette, Illinois: Bahá'í Publishing Trust, 1955.

Taherzadeh, Adib. *The Revelation of Bahá'u'lláh*. Oxford: George Ronald, vol. 2, 1977; vol. 3, 1983.

Universal House of Justice. Letter to the Followers of Bahá'u'lláh in the United States of America, 19 December 1988.

—— Memorandum on references in the *Synopsis and Codification of the Kitáb-i-Aqdas* which refer to the relative status of men and women, 5 August 1987.

—— Memorandum on the implications of the Bahá'í teachings regarding women, 8 October 1987.

Women. A compilation of the Research Department of the Universal House of Justice. Oakham: Bahá'í Publishing Trust, 1986.

References

Asking Questions

1. Keynes, *Sir Thomas Browne*, p. 17.
2. Shoghi Effendi, *World Order of Bahá'u'lláh*, p. 168.
3. Bahá'u'lláh, *Hidden Words*, Arabic no. 66.
4. ibid. Persian no. 77.
5. Bahá'u'lláh, *Gleanings*, CXIII, pp. 223–5.
6. ibid. LXXXIX, p. 176.
7. See, for example, Nabíl, *Dawn-Breakers*, p. 281.
8. ibid. p. 282.
9. Letter written on behalf of Shoghi Effendi, 30 August 1952. *Lights of Guidance*, no. 789, p. 237.
10. See Taherzadeh, *Revelation*, vol. 2, pp. 107–15.
11. Nabíl, *Dawn-Breakers*, p. 57.
12. ibid. p. 59.
13. ibid. pp. 104–6.
14. ibid. p. 106.
15. ibid.
16. ibid. pp. 69–70.
17. ibid. pp. 81–2.
18. ibid. p. 381.
19. ibid. pp. 134–6.
20. ibid. p. 202.
21. ibid. pp. 318–19.
22. ibid. pp. 172–4.
23. ibid. p. 469.

24. ibid. pp. 175–6.
25. Bahá'u'lláh, *Gleanings*, XCII, p. 183.

About Scholarship

1. Bahá'u'lláh, *Hidden Words*, Arabic no. 21.
2. ibid.
3. See 'Abdu'l-Bahá, *Memorials*, p. 200.
4. See Nabíl, *Dawn-Breakers*, pp. 162–8.
5. Mottahedeh, *Mantle of the Prophet*, p. 109.
6. Bahá'u'lláh, *Gleanings*, CXXX, p. 285.
7. Nabíl, *Dawn-Breakers*, p. 164.
8. Bahá'u'lláh, *Tablets*, p. 150.
9. Bahá'u'lláh, *Seven Valleys and Four Valleys*, p. 62.
10. Bahá'u'lláh, *Tablets*, p. 151.
11. Bahá'u'lláh, *Seven Valleys and Four Valleys*, p. 65.
12. See Nabíl, *Dawn-Breakers*, pp. 305–6.

Priestcraft

1. Shoghi Effendi, *God Passes By*, p. 33.
2. Nabíl, *Dawn-Breakers*, p. 292.
3. ibid. p. 294n.
4. Shoghi Effendi, *God Passes By*, pp. 31–2.
5. Nabíl, *Dawn-Breakers*, p. 293.
6. ibid. p. 294n.
7. ibid. p. 294.
8. ibid. p. 295.
9. ibid. p. 197.
10. ibid. p. 294.
11. ibid. p. 296.
12. ibid. p. 294.
13. Shoghi Effendi, *God Passes By*, p. 33.
14. ibid.

15. Nabíl, *Dawn-Breakers*, p. 294.
16. ibid. pp. 294–5.
17. ibid. p. 295.
18. ibid.
19. ibid.
20. ibid. p. 297.
21. ibid. p. 298.
22. ibid.

Fundamentalism

1. Rilke, *Notebooks*.
2. Langer, *Adolf Hitler*, p. 63.
3. ibid. p. 47.
4. ibid. p. 46.
5. Momen, *Bábí and Bahá'í Religions*, pp. 100–105.
6. Nabíl, *Dawn-Breakers*, p. 445.
7. ibid. p. 452.
8. ibid. p. 448.
9. ibid. pp. 448–9.
10. ibid. p. 453.
11. ibid. p. 454.
12. ibid. p. 458.
13. ibid. p. 459.
14. ibid. p. 460.
15. ibid. pp. 460–61.
16. ibid. p. 461.
17. ibid. p. 462.
18. ibid. p. 461.
19. ibid.
20. ibid. p. 462.
21. ibid. p. 453.
22. 'Abdu'l-Bahá, *Traveller's Narrative*, pp. 215–16.
23. Nabíl, *Dawn-Breakers*, pp. 462–3.

24. ibid. p. 463.
25. ibid.

Fear

1. See 'Abdu'l-Bahá, *Memorials*, pp. 108–16.
2. ibid. p. 114.
3. ibid. p. 115.
4. ibid. p. 116.
5. ibid.
6. Shoghi Effendi, *God Passes By*, pp. 32–3.
7. 'Abdu'l-Bahá, *Memorials*, p. 111.
8. ibid.
9. Midgley and Hughes, *Women's Choices*, p. 67.
10. ibid. p. 68.
11. 'Abdu'l-Bahá, *Memorials*, p. 177.
12. Nabíl, *Dawn-Breakers*, p. 385n.
13. 'Abdu'l-Bahá, *Memorials*, p. 177.
14. 'wrapped their heads in their robes to keep themselves from gazing on the face of her Highness the Pure One'. A.L.M. Nicolas, quoted in Nabíl, *Dawn-Breakers*, p. 294n.
15. ibid. p. 297.
16. ibid. p. 295.
17. Shoghi Effendi, *God Passes By*, p. 33.
18. ibid. pp. 32–3.
19. ibid. pp. 33–4.
20. 'Abdu'l-Bahá, *Selections*, p. 172.

Freedom

1. Letter of the Universal House of Justice, 29 December 1988.
2. ibid.

3. ibid.
4. 'Abdu'l-Bahá, *Memorials*, p. 34.
5. Taherzadeh, *Revelation*, vol. 3, p. 177n.
6. ibid. p. 177.
7. Letter of the Universal House of Justice, 29 December 1988.
8. Taherzadeh, *Revelation*, vol. 3, p. 176.
9. 'Abdu'l-Bahá, *Memorials*, p. 34.
10. Bahá'u'lláh, *Gleanings*, CLI, pp. 319–20.
11. Letter of the Universal House of Justice, 29 December 1988.
12. Taherzadeh, *Revelation*, vol. 3, p. 186.
13. Letter of the Universal House of Justice, 29 December 1988.
14. ibid.
15. Shoghi Effendi, *World Order of Bahá'u'lláh*, p. 152.
16. Letter of the Universal House of Justice, 29 December 1988.
17. ibid.
18. ibid.
19. Taherzadeh, *Revelation*, vol. 3, pp. 183–4.
20. ibid.
21. Letter of the Universal House of Justice, 29 December 1988.

Women

1. Browne, *Materials*, p. 330.
2. Shoghi Effendi, *Call to the Nations*, p. 15.
3. See Nabíl, *Dawn-Breakers*, pp. 383–5n.
4. ibid. p. 434.
5. Bahá'u'lláh, *Kitáb-i-Íqán*, p. 149.
6. See 'Abdu'l-Bahá, *Selections*, pp. 176–7.

7. From an anecdote told by Laura to Mark Hofman in 1971.
8. Balyuzi, *'Abdu'l-Bahá*, p. 83.
9. 'Abdu'l-Bahá, *Some Answered Questions*, p. vi.
10. Dreyfus-Barney, 'Only a Word', p. 667.
11. ibid.
12. Recollection of Joyce Dahl, in a letter to the author.
13. Balyuzi, *'Abdu'l-Bahá*, pp. 83–4.
14. 'Abdu'l-Bahá, *Some Answered Questions*, p. v.
15. ibid. p. 246.
16. ibid. p. v.

And the Law

1. Bahá'u'lláh, *Gleanings*, CLV, pp. 332–3.
2. From untranslated Tablets at the Bahá'í World Centre.
3. Bahá'u'lláh, *Hidden Words*, Persian no. 40.
4. ibid. Persian no. 14.
5. Memorandum of the Universal House of Justice, 8 October 1987.
6. Memorandum of the Universal House of Justice, 5 August 1987.
7. Cited in ibid.
8. ibid.
9. Shoghi Effendi, *Call to the Nations*, p. 11.
10. Bahá'u'lláh, *Synopsis and Codification*, p. 61.
11. Memorandum of the Universal House of Justice, 5 August 1987.
12. Bahá'u'lláh, *Hidden Words*, Persian no. 81.
13. ibid. Persian no. 80.
14. ibid. Persian no. 82.
15. Letter of the Universal House of Justice, 28 April 1974, cited in *Women*, p. 13.
16. Bahá'u'lláh, *Gleanings*, LX, p. 118.

17. Bahá'u'lláh, *Synopsis and Codification*, p. 39.
18. Memorandum of the Universal House of Justice, 8 October 1987.
19. Letter of the Universal House of Justice, 24 July 1975, cited in *Women*, p. 13.
20. 'Abdu'l-Bahá, cited in ibid. p. 14.
21. Memorandum of the Universal House of Justice, 5 August 1987.
22. The Universal House of Justice, Introduction to *Synopsis and Codification*, p. 6.
23. Memorandum of the Universal House of Justice, 5 August 1987.